Finance and Manage Your Life: A Planning Guide for Generation Y

James S. West, Ph.D.

In collaboration with
Brianne Bilsky, Ph.D.

Copyediting by Brianne Bilsky, Ph. D.
Cover designed by Christian Griffith

Disclaimer: This publication contains opinions, ideas, and suggestions of the author who is not an accountant, certified financial planner, financial advisor, lawyer, or psychologist, thus is not providing financial, legal, investment, accounting, psychological or any other professional service or advice. As indicated in the content, if readers desire specific professional services and/or advice on any topic covered in this publication, they should consult qualified experts in the appropriate field.

ACKNOWLEDGEMENTS

I want to thank all the Gen Y college students I have had in my business administration classes, particularly those who were my advisees and the graduates who have stayed in touch with me over the years. You keep me young, at least in my own mind, and always remind me why I chose to be a college professor, with no regrets.

I also want to acknowledge the inspiration my sons Stephen and Bradley provided for many of the topics presented in this book. Everything I do is with the two of you in my mind and heart.

CONTENTS

1. Introduction

Myth: "I'm young, so I don't need to worry about this yet."

This book was written specifically for you, Generation Y—sometimes called the "Millennials," or what a Pew Center Report called "Generation Next"—who are recent high school, technical school, or college graduates who have entered the workforce. [10] Admittedly, most life planning and financial planning books are aimed at older people who are in the middle of their careers and lives; people who may already be in financial trouble and looking desperately for helpful suggestions. Many, if not most, older people do need help from a reliable source; however, the real problem with financial and life planning is that we do not teach these skills to young people *before* they get into trouble. More troublesome is that most self–help books, many financial planners, as well as "life coaches" typically fail to point out the close connection between successful financial planning and other life-management skills.

There are some middle and high school courses that touch on a few of these subjects, but they are usually elective offerings, often taken for an easy grade or as a "filler" course, not because students really think they need this information. In fact, as with most issues, the ones who need it the most are probably the least likely to choose such a course on their own. No high school I know of requires such a course, but they should. Unfortunately, few teachers at that level have the education or expertise to teach such courses without significant retooling.

If we learned to plan our lives early on, we could avoid some of the troubles that haunt many people when they get older: overwhelming debt, little or no savings for emergencies, inadequate plans for retirement, as well as failure to financially plan for the "good things" they desire in life. For example: having and raising children, vacations, buying a house or condo, a summer home, new cars, post-secondary education or training for their kids (or themselves), etc. Worst of all, young people often have no clear, specific and measurable life goals and objectives that could help guide their life and career as well as their personal finances, all too often just accepting their family's well-intentioned, but possibly misguided, notions of "what you should do." For example, those readers who are in college, or recently graduated from college, should ask themselves when and why they decided to go to college.

Myth: "Everyone should go to college."

Approximately 65% of Gen Y-ers go to college (though roughly half graduate). [18] Most college-bound students are actively involved in the decision on *which* college to attend, but few ask themselves *if they should go*—or, if they should go right out of high school. Ever wonder why? After all, there are a lot of alternatives: entering the workforce to gain work experience (and possibly to save money to pay for further education), military duty (and possibly training that could lead to a civilian job later), apprenticeship in a skilled trade, enrolling in a technical/vocational school to learn a specific skill or trade, or "finding yourself" while helping the less fortunate (e.g., joining the Peace Corps or AmeriCorps, etc.).

In most cases you, and especially your parents, just assumed you would go to college without considering whether that was really the right thing for you, or the thing to do right after high school. This is something that has been going on for several generations—most notably starting with the "Baby Boomer" generation. The myth is perpetuated by societal (especially political) leaders who often state, "everyone should have a chance to go to college," but usually without the proper qualification: "if that is what is best for you and what YOU want to do." We don't need a society full of college graduates without the accompanying people who can do the many skilled jobs that make our society work; people who not only are good at those jobs but also really enjoy that type of work. Today, and for the foreseeable future, the greatest shortage of workers in the U.S. is skilled workers (not college grads): mechanics of all kinds, plumbers, electricians, computer technicians, nurses, medical technicians, etc. In 2011 and

2012, while politicians blamed each other for a high unemployment rate, over 3.5 million well-paying skilled jobs in the U.S. went unfilled due to a lack of qualified applicants. [1] This wasn't just a jobs problem; it was a shortage of skilled labor problem (combined with too many unskilled workers whose jobs have been replaced with newer, low cost technology).

I'm not sure we could even calculate the value of resources devoted to the college education of young people who underperform in school, don't really know what they want to do when they graduate, why they chose their particular major, and who are highly likely to end up in a career that has little if anything to do with what they studied in college. Yes, there is the possibility that some students are there just to learn how to learn, but most college professors can attest to the fact that those students are few and far between (though many college presidents and deans, particularly those at liberal arts colleges, often point to this as the best reason to attend college). Of course, college administrators have a vested interest in getting young people to want to go to college (even public colleges and universities count on tuition to help finance their operating expenses), and politicians, well they usually say anything that will help them get elected!

To the credit of a few of these "leaders," we are starting to hear some talk about the importance of considering non-college options. Certainly, the cost of non-college, post-high school training and education options are usually less than the cost of four-year colleges and universities, but that should not be the only reason to consider this path. It should be based on what will best help young adults achieve their goals—based on a well thought out personal life plan.

Not only should young people start asking themselves what kind of post-high school education they need to accomplish their goals, but we all should start asking ourselves why more young people haven't questioned this in the past. We may collectively be responsible for this. As a society, we attach status and prestige to a college education much more than we do to the other forms of post-high school training/education. We continue to do this at our societal peril, given the serious shortage of highly skilled labor that the U.S. is already experiencing, while also having a worrisome increase in unskilled workers for whom, due to new technologies, there will permanently be fewer and fewer jobs (economists refer to this as structural unemployment).

At the same time, young people who choose to get a job after completing high school, attend a vocational/technical school, or join the military, etc. (i.e., all those who do not go to college) also need to ask themselves why they chose the route they did. Did they consider other options such as going to college, or did they dismiss that possibility without thoroughly investigating their ability to gain admission and find funding for a college education? While it is clear that some college students should probably have taken a different post-high school path, one in which they would be happier and with a greater chance of success, we also should ask if there are young people who took a non-college path who would have been happier and more successful had they gone to college and pursued a career which required that credential. Ultimately, both situations reflect a lack of planning by many young people, failing to question which post-high school route would provide the best opportunity to achieve their career and life goals. In too many cases, young adults and their families have simply assumed what route would be taken after high school, without ever considering and investigating other options, not to mention clarifying the young adult's personal goals in life.

Myth: "Your parents should help do the planning."

Most parents, whether or not they have learned to plan their own lives and finances, often fail to teach their children to plan for themselves. Our society has evolved (some would say devolved) to one in which many parents so indulge their children that they effectively do all the planning and decision-making for them. Many parents decide what activities their child should participate in, drive them to and from each event, attend all events, and practice with them. The same is often true for academic as well as extracurricular activities: parents tutor their children; quiz them prior to exams; and fight their battles when there is a disagreement of proper performance evaluation. Some parents even badger schools until their child is in the "right class" or has the "best teacher."

This pervasive involvement in their children's lives doesn't stop at high school graduation. Some studies have indicated that college students talk to their parents on an average of 13 times a week, which is not exactly "going away" to school in the traditional sense, and call even more often after they graduate. In addition, approximately 30% of college students regularly email drafts of term papers home for their parents to edit before submitting them to their professors. [7] College administrators have actually developed plans for dealing with what are often called "helicopter parents"—those who constantly "hover" over their children's activities. [19] While at first glance this may seem nice, even supportive (and in all likelihood well-meaning), it also allows the parents to continue in the role of planner and decision-maker, with their children in the role of, well, children who either do what they are told, or not, but *who are not planning their own lives*!

Parents clearly need to have an advisory and supportive role in their children's lives after high school, but that should be preceded by teaching their children to plan their own lives *before* they are on their own, even allowing them to make their own decisions and learn from their mistakes. Parents who are there to help their kids when they really need it is OK, but doing the planning and decision-making for them is NOT! Some parents who allow, or even encourage, their children to come back and live at home after their post-high school education/training may be helping them get a good start in their career or save money to eventually be able to live on their own, or they just might be furthering their child's lack of independence. Sometimes it may simply be a way for the parents to keep their kids at home a while longer, usually as much or more for the parents' benefit than that of their now-adult child. If parents want to help their adult children in a meaningful way, then they should encourage them to be on their own, learning to manage their own lives, with their parents in the background available to help when necessary as a safety net.

Truth: "You need to plan your own life."

As young adults, YOU need to start taking on planning and decision-making for yourselves, even if your parents are willing to or insist on doing this for you. At the same time, listen to your parents' advice (and seriously consider what they have to say since they have probably been there/done that for most planning issues you will be facing), but ultimately, you need to make your own decisions. Furthermore, while most parents will be happy to be a safety net if something goes wrong, that kindness only should be used as a last resort, particularly regarding financial wants (which are very different than needs). Part of a life plan should be learning to live on your own, even embracing the idea of becoming "responsibly independent." You can think of this as sort of kicking yourself out of the nest.

However, if you have to return home to live with your parents because of a poor job market or having lost a job, you should recognize that you are not alone. Over 33% of people who are under 34 years of age are in the same situation. [28] It certainly can be a blow to your self esteem, but if you use this as an opportunity to find a good job, gain admission to graduate school or some other form of advanced training, or save money in order to get a better start when you are, once again, out on your own, then you and your parents might want to consider this an "early inheritance." This can turn into a good short-term life plan, but only if you: 1. have a specific plan of action, including a time frame to achieve your objectives; and 2. get a part-time or temporary full-time job to help pay what you can afford in rent and food costs, as well as contributing to the household by doing your share of chores. The latter will probably garner you more time leeway living at home until you achieve your near-term objectives and will help you regain any lost self-confidence and sense of self worth that may have been damaged by circumstances beyond your control.

For those Gen Y readers who are or hope to be parents some day, please take note of the above so that you can begin to break the all-too-typical cycle of parents doing too much planning and decision-making for their kids as they develop and grow into adulthood. Hopefully, you will continue to provide a safety net for your children when needed, but also encourage them to do whatever is necessary to be able to live on their own.

Truth: "Nothing worthwhile is easy."

Yes, that is an old saying. However, it also happens to usually be true. In addition to being a society that fails to teach young people to plan, the United States has become a society with a "quick fix" mentality. If hungry, we want food served in seconds, and expect it to be warm, reasonably fresh and taste good. We want "no-workout" diets that take 10-20 pounds off as soon as possible; weight caused in part, no doubt, by our appetite for fast food and lack of real exercise. We purchase "miracle" products to help us get in shape with little or no effort, so we can continue a sedate lifestyle while toning our abs. We watch and listen to TV and radio shows where some pop psychologist gives us quick answers to solve personal and relationship problems that were years in the making.

We appear to be ready at every turn to listen to anyone who can give us "no pain" or "no struggle" quick answers to our everyday problems. We rarely bother to ask about the credentials of these people whom we trust to provide "quick-fix answers" to life's important questions. In many cases, they have no more expertise than the readers or listeners to whom they are preaching; or these experts' backgrounds may have nothing to do with the area in which they are offering advice. We also seem not to be bothered by inconsistent or overly simplistic advice given by some of these *supposed experts*.

Don't feel alone; business professionals also appear to be susceptible to the "quick fix" syndrome. They read books telling them how to learn to manage their organizations in a few minutes, or how to be an effective leader in a few easy steps. "Wannabe" business tycoons read, listen and watch the latest self-help gurus who tell them how to become millionaires in a few months with little or no effort, and even less money (failing to point out that the best way to become that millionaire is probably to be the one selling the hot, quick-fix-of-the-day seminars, DVDs and books).

Sorry, but the quick fix rarely works well. It may temporarily suffice, but all the little-used exercise machines and devices that reside in garages, sheds, and attics or have been discarded on the curb are a testament to the futility of many "easy" answers for achieving the perfect body. The vast number (a majority) of dieters regain their lost weight, and end up adding to their waistlines, offering an additional exhibit for the public display of idolatry to the "quick fix" gods, fueling a multi-billion dollar diet industry. And, indeed, they are false gods. Even for those few quick fixes that actually seem to work (Viagra and other ED remedies for your parents' generation come to mind), there is a legal process to obtain the product, there may be physical as well as financial consequences, and, for some products, we don't really know the long term health effects—at least not yet! And don't forget the millions, if not billions, of dollars lost annually by individuals scammed into paying for those "get rich quick" seminars, books and DVDs.

We shouldn't confuse convenience with a quick fix. But, we should recognize the price we have to pay for convenience. Just check out the price differences between your corner convenience store and the supermarket. There is nothing wrong with seeking convenient ways to complete chores or even to achieve an important life goal; we just have to remember that it may have a downside. For example, getting a college degree online may be more convenient and, for some, the only way to do it. However, this approach may take a much longer time to get a degree (and schools that offer such programs often have a much lower graduation rate than brick and mortar schools), and many employers may not value that form of higher education as much as they do more traditional schools. You also may lose something by not interacting on a personal basis with faculty and other students. But, if we assess the pros and cons and make decisions having weighed all the facts, that is not the same as blindly falling for the many easy, quick-fix or more convenient solutions usually offered with no negative consequences pointed out—at least not in big print. For example, if prospective online education students understand the pitfalls of this approach, they can make a better decision on when and where to pursue this method of obtaining a degree.

The above warning also applies to those young people who consider signing up for one of the new free "massive open online courses" (MOOC) being offered from some well-known schools to anyone (worldwide) with Internet access. [5] Such a course may provide a good learning experience (though the jury is still out on this education delivery method), but even those courses that offer a "certificate of successful completion" may not be seen as sufficient training by prospective employers seeking specific kinds of proficiency or who expect more traditional methods of certification. This is not to say that a MOOC experience won't be helpful for your career, but it would be wise to check it out carefully before signing up for such a class. The same is true for some of the specific skill development "boot camps" that are popping up for both college grads and non-college grads, some of which only charge a fee after their students get a job in the designated skill area. [21] These unique training programs may be the wave of the future, but you should enroll in such programs only after careful thought and with realistic expectations.

Financial planning is no different than planning the other important aspects of our lives. There is no easy answer or quick path to financial security and independence, and we should not be satisfied with just keeping our heads above water. It's more complicated than that. As with most things in life, you can't solve one dilemma without looking at the impact of your behavior on all other aspects of your life. For example, you may not be able to avoid health problems without doing something about the stress in your life, which in turn may have been caused, at least in part, by money problems.

Quick-Fix Alert!

Any time you see a self-help book or article in a magazine with the following words or phrases, immediately discard it, or minimally realize it is probably not the best advice:

- Easy steps
- Fast
- No pain
- One minute (or any short time period) solution
- No effort required
- Results guaranteed

You get the idea!

Truth: "Financial planning requires a holistic life approach."

Do you remember hearing the old saying "the whole is greater than the sum of its parts"? While most of us have heard that cliché, we haven't taken the time to think about what it really means—namely, that you can't achieve the whole (whatever that is) unless all the parts are present and working together in a complimentary manner. For the purposes of this book, the whole is *your life*; what most of us would probably define as a happy and rewarding life with few, if any, regrets. Your finances are only *one* part of that whole life.

Quite simply (well, actually, there is nothing simple about it), you should not worry about your finances without looking carefully at the other major parts of your life. You certainly cannot plan for financial security and independence without taking care of and planning for all the other parts of the whole. Of course, the rest of the story is that you also cannot, in most cases, plan well for the other parts of your life without being concerned about your personal finances. Even monks who voluntarily live their entire adult lives in a remote monastery have financial needs that must be taken care of by someone.

While the focus of this book is ultimately on personal financial planning, we will look carefully at how that subject intertwines with the other important parts of our lives such as our physical environment, personal well-being, use of time, and personal goals and objectives, including desired career. Of course, personal well-being is a big subject, but we will deal with it as one of the components of your life that affects and is affected by your personal finances. This is the "holistic" approach—and anything but a quick fix!

Myth: "Anyone who writes and publishes a book must be an expert."

Always question the expertise of an author or speaker. What are their academic credentials, and do they have experience in the field they are writing or talking about? If not, they are just offering opinions, and you should take what they say with a grain of salt, not as expertise.

A person doesn't need to have a graduate degree, or even a bachelor's degree, to claim expertise on a particular topic, but it helps. Why? Well, because it indicates that they have studied the topic extensively, not just developed some opinions (probably unsubstantiated) over time. "What about experience?" you might also ask. Experience can be very helpful, but, by itself, doesn't mean anything. It might have been a bad experience, or unique to that individual, and may not be able to be generalized to the behavior of others. We need to ask: what kind of experience, how much, and was it based on a developed expertise through practice or just based on self-proclaimed wisdom? Some "unnamed" public figures come to mind: one author and radio/TV personality offers personal relationship advice but comes to us via a doctorate in physiology (not in psychology). Other media personalities who offer advice on almost everything come to us with expertise that is totally self-proclaimed, with no specific training to speak of and very little education. Their advice may be entertaining, and we may admire their ability at self promotion if not self-aggrandizement, but we should take their advice and points of view with more than one grain of salt!

So, you might be asking: what are THIS author's credentials for writing a book to tell others how to manage their money, not to mention their lives? Well, I have lived longer than most of you, so I am experienced. I am not wealthy, but I am financially secure. I was able to take early retirement at a relatively young age and could have chosen not to work and still survive financially without dramatically altering my lifestyle, but I didn't. I found a new career. I have a Ph.D. in Business Administration, a Masters degree specializing in Economics, and I have taught courses in marketing and management at the collegiate level for many years. A few years ago I became particularly interested in personal financial management, noting how poorly most people handle their finances and how little attention is paid to this subject in higher education. However, the more I looked into this subject, the more I realized it could not be separated from other life skills. Ultimately, I used the combination of my formal training and personal experience to develop and teach a course on life-management skills, with an emphasis on personal financial planning. The latter is where I developed and refined many ideas for this book and its focus on your generation.

In addition, I was fortunate to secure the assistance of Brianne Bilsky, a Ph.D. in English who is a member of Generation Y and who works as an administrator in the Student Life Office at a U.S. college, to help edit this book and collaborate on identifying the kinds of issues that are likely to be pertinent to the intended Gen Y audience.

Truth: "You cannot afford to procrastinate."

The sooner you begin to plan your life, the sooner you will be ready to develop a plan for the money to finance that life. Remember, you cannot afford to wait until you are 40 or 50 years old to start, though many people do. While it certainly is better to start late than never, those ten to twenty years of lost time can be very costly in terms of achieving career goals, financial well-being, personal and family lifestyle, the ability to choose when to retire, or to start a second or even third career. Our ever-increasing lifespan might make it seem less imperative to start as soon as our predecessors, but living longer is neither guaranteed nor inexpensive. (Remember, average life expectancy is just that—an *average*.)

Although they differ on exact amounts and ages, most credible sources on financial planning suggest that you should have saved increasing multiples of your current salary at various age levels. For example, at least twice your annual income in savings and investments by age 40; 4 times your salary by age 50; and 8-12 times by retirement age. [14] We probably should add a pre-40 goal of having at least 6 months of regular expenses in a liquid savings account by age 30-39 to protect you from either a loss of job or to facilitate looking for a new job and having time to arrange moving from one location to another if necessary. Of course, if you decided to obtain advanced education or training, you will need to modify these age-specific targets. But don't worry too much. As part of Gen Y, you are also likely to live longer than previous generations!

The ideal time to start life planning is in your very early years, even as young as 9 or 10—handling your allowance responsibly— but that requires parents to help initiate the planning by creating an environment where planning becomes part of your normal life behavior. Obviously, if you're reading this book, you're probably well beyond those early training years, but starting to plan in your late teens or early 20s, even 30s, is still a vast improvement over previous generations who often started in their late 40s, 50s, or, in many cases, never at all. The later we start, the less time we have to achieve our goals and the more likely we won't stick to a plan because of the bad habits we may have already developed; thus requiring us to "unlearn" those bad habits as well as to learn and begin good ones.

Who and What are Generation Y?

Apparently there is no specific agreement on who exactly should be included in the Generation Y designation, but most sources consulted suggest that they are people who were born in the late 70's to early 80's through the late 90's (those born after that are sometimes referred to as Generation Z). Generation Y are young people approximately 18-34 years of age, sometimes referred to as the "Millennials," "Generation Next," "Generation

We," or, "Echo Boomers" due to the very large number of people who fall into this grouping (approximately 75 million Americans), the largest population demographic group since the Baby Boomers. [17] Apparently, your generation is confusing everyone (or, more likely, the different labels used reflect author "gimmicks" to publish and gain attention to their books or articles).

Some behavioral descriptions of Generation Y include:

- Happy and optimistic about life.
- See yourselves as unique and distinct.
- Want to become rich and famous.
- Very tolerant on issues such as immigration, race, and homosexuality.
- Technologically savvy.
- Use social media extensively.
- Are willing and able to multitask.
- Maintain close contact with family and friends.
- Self-motivated.
- Very mobile.
- Not as actively religious as previous generations.
- Less cynical about the role of government. [10]

Some authors might add financial illiteracy to this list, and of course, there are other behavioral descriptors of Generation Y pertaining to recreational drug use, casual sex, etc. that do not pertain directly to this book so best to leave them out. However, it is also true that the above list does not apply to everyone in Gen Y. These clearly are generalizations based on the self-perceptions of Generation Y. But, such generalizations can still help provide a "big picture" of your generation.

However, the behavioral profile of Generation Y fails to point out that you are also going to be the most nationally indebted generation (not your own debt, but the country's indebtedness). The U.S. birthrate is at an historic low, and we continue to thwart immigration, which means your generation will have to take the primary role in dealing with the longer-living elderly and their many financial and healthcare needs. At the same time, this will be a country with too few younger people to take care of your needs when you reach retirement age.

In addition, our public school education system is broken, and our once exalted higher education system is increasingly being scrutinized not only for dramatically increasing costs, but for its ineffectiveness in providing the education needed. This means that the current shortage of skilled labor will continue to grow, leaving a larger and larger number of unemployable unskilled workers, which in turn will lead to a crisis, politically, socially, and economically.

The above may not seem to be directly relevant for this book on life and financial planning for Generation Y, but the direction your country takes does affect you. It indicates not only some issues to consider when engaged in career planning, but also the importance of planning for your own future and not counting on state or federal government help—making your financial planning more crucial to your future than it was for your parents or grandparents.

2. The Money Problem
Warning: This may not be a comforting section to read.

Most of us do not manage our money very well, and the evidence is irrefutable. All we have to do is look at consumer debt, bankruptcy rates, mortgage foreclosures, savings rates, and estimates of the number of middle-aged people who have inadequately prepared for retirement. Until the "great recession" that began, in earnest, around 2007/2008 (many of the conditions that led to that problem started earlier), many of us were saving at or near a negative rate, which is a nice way of saying we were routinely spending more money than we earned, thus reducing our previous savings or acquiring more and more debt. [12]

Consumer Debt

Sixty to seventy years ago, the only people who would easily qualify for credit or bank loans were, as the old saying goes, those who could prove they didn't need them; in other words, they had collateral worth more than the amount they were borrowing. And, while credit has been more difficult to get during the deep recession mentioned above, today credit cards are offered to almost everyone 18 and over regardless of employment or credit history (credit rating/score). A low credit score is more likely to have the consequence of a higher interest rate rather than denial of credit or loans from financial institutions. At first glance, this may seem like a consumer-friendly trend, but it allows people to develop very poor financial habits, ending up paying a lot more for the durable goods they buy on credit and often amassing a level of debt that is unsustainable.

Although **household debt** has declined from its 2007 all time high due to the "great recession," it is still troublesome (non-mortgage household debt in 2010 for households headed by people

35 and under was approximately $15,500, much of which was in the form of credit card debt). [23] Younger cardholders, particularly those with low credit ratings, often pay an outrageous interest rate on credit cards, as high as 18-21% per year, with some never paying off their balances and barely able to make their minimum payment each month. The situation is worsened by the fact that many people have 3 or more bankcards, not to mention a wallet or purse full of individual department store and gas credit cards. Since most of those cards allow the customer to carry over the balance from one payment period to another and, dangerously, to use one card to pay the minimum balance due on other cards, this can become a very rocky road that easily can lead to serious if not ruinous financial problems.

College loans and other school-related debt has become a major social issue regarding the value of attending college. Graduates embark on their first career job with an average credit card debt of over $4,000, not to mention their college loans, which average nearly $23,000 upon graduation. [23, 26] The latter, in many cases, are justified as an investment and usually have much lower interest rates than other types of loans or credit, but the amount owed by students upon graduation has increased substantially, corresponding with the skyrocketing cost of higher education. While not currently a focus of the media, graduate and professional school debt is often an even greater burden than undergraduate college debt for those who pursue advanced degrees, particularly for programs that do not offer tuition waivers and/or stipends in the form of assistantships or fellowships. While some master's degree programs and most Ph.D. programs offer such assistance, many people attending medical school, dental school, and law school are responsible for finding or borrowing funds for such training. Graduate school debt can be as much as $50,000 for a master's degree (much more for some high-end MBA degrees), $36,000 for a Ph.D. (even though these degrees often include assistantships and tuition waivers), and well over $100,000 for professional degrees in medicine, veterinary medicine, and some law schools. [9]

Today, **auto loan** payments can be spread over 3-6 years, allowing people to purchase a more expensive car than they could otherwise afford or to minimize the monthly payment amount required on a more affordable car. [25] The latter allows the borrower to spend their money on other things, but the additional interest they have to pay on their longer loans dramatically increases the cost of the car they bought. The popularity of leasing cars rather than buying them has actually made things more complicated—and maybe worse—allowing consumers to further reduce the monthly payment but have no equity in the car at the end of their lease, allowing them to drive a nicer car than they can actually afford, or, again, reducing monthly payments so that they have more money to spend on other things they want. As we will discuss later, leasing a car could be an effective strategy, but only if thought out carefully and as part of a total life plan.

Home mortgages may even be more troublesome. Until the home mortgage market collapse that began in 2007, there were an ever-increasing number of "creative methods" available to average middle class customers for financing the purchase of a house that they could not otherwise afford. Does the phrase "house poor" ring a bell? Consumers have been offered 30-year loans for a number of years, but suddenly there were some 35+ year loans available, or low-payment loans with a big balloon payment at the end of 5 to 10 years, adjustable rate mortgages (ARMs) with no caps, or interest-only loans (by far the worst of all methods for most buyers), just to name a few.

All of these creative financing methods allowed homebuyers to live large and pay later. However, when home values plummeted, many people found their homes were worth less than what they owed on their mortgage loans, which was the beginning of the collapse of the housing market and the financial ruin of thousands of homeowners. Of course, this could be even worse for those homebuyers who accept an adjustable rate mortgage. If their interest rates go up as the value of their home decreases, the homeowners could find themselves in serious financial difficulty. Banks facilitated this questionable buyer behavior by approving mortgages for 5 times annual family income when just a few years earlier they normally limited mortgage amounts to 3 times annual income. Many homebuyers were getting "no money down" offers from home loan institutions. Far too many people used these methods to get into a house that was more than they could afford, and, ultimately, this contributed to serious financial difficulties. Minimally, it seriously restricted consumers' ability to meet goals in other areas of their life (such as eating!). Is it ever a good idea to accept creative financing for a major purchase? Sure, but once again, it has to be part of a well thought out financial plan, which we'll talk much more about later in the book.

A typical excuse for accepting a mortgage larger than might be wise was that you can grow into the mortgage; as your income increases, your payments will be easier to handle. That may have been possible in past times, but most middle income people have had no "real" growth and possibly actual reductions in their "real income" over the past 5 to 10 years. There are no guarantees of rising income, and, depending on the type of mortgage, the cost of financing may also increase over time. We also are told that homeowners can build equity over time, even if they have to struggle to meet payments for a while. But, again, there is no guarantee of rising home values. The home mortgage foreclosure and "walk-away" debacle in 2008-2009 was accompanied by, and in some cases caused by, dramatic declines in average home values in many, if not most, U.S. housing markets. The most dramatic declines were in what had been labeled earlier as the "hottest" real estate areas in the U.S. (Las Vegas and most cities in Florida come to mind).

And all of this happened despite plenty of warnings. In 2006 and 2007, numerous financial and real estate analysts suggested that houses were vastly overpriced (a housing "bubble") in many markets and that an economic downturn could easily burst that bubble, with house values tumbling. They also warned that, in other geographical regions, the growth of home values might not plummet, but could become stagnant or grow very slowly. In hindsight, those were very prophetic warnings that became accurate predictions.

Could a buyer "luck out" as many West Coast homeowners did during the 1990s when home values increased dramatically? Sure, but we now know you should not count on luck. That is a sure-fire way to find yourself in financial trouble, and possibly back home living with your parents, your in-laws or, worse, homeless.

Note

Don't worry! Advice on what to do about money problems is coming a bit later, but in the meantime, you might be able to learn from mistakes made by your parents' and grandparents' generation.

Bankruptcies and Foreclosures

There were approximately 1,180,000 non-business bankruptcies filed in 2012, providing more evidence that we haven't handled our money very well. [30] Clearly, we each are primarily responsible for our own debt circumstances, but we're not totally to blame. No one strongly encourages us to learn how to manage our money until we're in financial trouble. Most educational courses on this subject are optional and not taken by most students in high school, and even fewer students in college. Again, we increasingly resort to what seems like the easy fix: filing bankruptcy as a first rather than final resort, a practice formerly reserved for the well-to-do but increasingly a popular means for the middle class to get out of financial difficulty. Sadly, until some recent changes in bankruptcy laws, there were troubling signs that bankruptcy had moved into the "in vogue" category, particularly in those states (such as Florida) that had very consumer-friendly (minimum consequence) bankruptcy rules. But let's not kid ourselves: there are always consequences to our behavior. In this case, both credit availability and self-esteem may suffer for many years.

Low Rate of Savings

At the beginning of the "great recession" of 2007-2009, the savings rate among U.S. citizens had dropped to its lowest point in modern times (the lowest it has been since the Great Depression), and much lower than most other industrialized nations. [20] This is not a compliment to our society, rather a significant internal weakness in the U.S. economy. However, this is a personal problem as well as a national one. The economic slowdown in the early 2000s certainly didn't help, and the deep recession in more recent years put many families "over the cliff" financially, exacerbated by millions of lost jobs and further worsened by many (actually, most) families in America not having sufficient savings to carry them beyond a month or two without starting to default on payment for credit cards, car loans, as well as the mortgages on their house.

However, by 2012, the American people who still had jobs actually started saving at a higher rate than they had prior to the recession; a rate of 3.3%. [6] While this was good for them, unfortunately it was bad for economic recovery that has traditionally been fueled by consumers' spending. The big question is, will this financial prudence continue after the recession? Sure, it can, but it probably won't.

We are a hedonistic society that wants immediate gratification in all areas of life. We borrow rather than save for luxury items. We even describe as basic needs what most of the world sees as wants or even luxuries. What young person doesn't have ten reasons why a cell phone (probably a "smart phone") is absolutely necessary today, usually leading off with the "safety" issue (then proceeds to drive while using the cell phone to talk or text)? And, what American family wouldn't feel deprived not to have at least a DVD player, if not a DVR? But how many of us could live for 6 months without a paycheck if we lost our job (even if we have a significant other who has a job), suddenly became disabled, or a myriad of other unforeseen financial crises that hit people every day?

Without a reasonable amount of savings we may lose more than the all-important financial safety net that savings provides; we also may lose out on unforeseen opportunities for investment, relocating to find a better job, re-training to gain new skills, finishing college or going to graduate school, etc. Moreover, the stress of living from paycheck-to-paycheck can take a tremendous toll on our psychological as well as physical health, not to mention relationships.

It would be a shame if Gen Y doesn't learn an important lesson from the "great recession" and make an effort to return to the 1970-1979 U.S. consumers' savings rate of over 9%. [20] In the long run it would be good for both the country's financial health as well as your personal financial well-being.

Inadequate Retirement Planning
Myth: "You won't have to worry about retirement for years."

Retirement is one of the most important financial issues for which we inadequately plan and, thus, save too little. Some estimates suggest that as many as 40% of Americans have no retirement savings, with 38% not even having an emergency fund. [29] Thus it seems safe to say that many, if not most, Americans have not developed any specific retirement plans, and may be solely relying on Social Security, a program which may not exist in its present form when these people actually retire. In any case, Social Security will not allow most people to retire anywhere near their pre-retirement standard of living—making their retirement years more bleak than golden. Of course, retirement planning involves much more than the amount of money you will have to live on after retirement. It has as much to do with the expenses you will be incurring (e.g., house payments, other debts, dependents, and your desired post-retirement lifestyle).

As with all life planning, retirement is not something you can afford to put off planning until you are in your 50s. You need to start planning for retirement with acceptance of your first career job, though probably not a subject that you should bring up during job interviews. Prospective employers may interpret such questions more in terms of your interest in quitting work as soon as possible rather than a conscientious concern for panning for your financial future.

Personal retirement planning has taken on even greater importance for people of all ages as more and more employers move to end or freeze their employer-sponsored defined-benefit pension plans in favor of tax-deferred employee-funded 401k-type programs. In many, but certainly not all cases, employers offer some percentage of matching contribution, but there is no guarantee that an employer's matching funds will continue forever. These trends shift the burden and risks of financing retirement more squarely on the shoulders of employees.

3. The Dire Consequences of Financial Problems

Having enough money does not, by itself, create happiness. But not having enough money can cause misery and even death. Money problems cause stress-related physical and psychological health problems as well as personal relationship difficulties, work problems, and unhappiness.

Stress

Stress may well be a major underlying cause of illness and unhappiness in modern society. There is significant evidence in medical studies that stress not only leads to periodic mental distress, but also can lead to serious mental illness. Physical illness can be caused by stress as well. While most people associate stress with stomach ulcers, they may not be aware that a high level of stress in your life actually can cause cancer (or at least lower your resistance to various cancers and other debilitating, if not deadly diseases). Minimally, stress may contribute to the onset of diseases that might have remained dormant without the catalyst of high stress. And, of course, money problems are one of the biggest causes of stress in our lives. We worry about paying the bills, about having enough money for unexpected expenses and emergencies, not to mention living the lifestyle that we desire, that we always thought we would live, or that we see others living.

Marital and Family Problems

Money difficulties, and the stress related to it, often are cited as a major cause of marital problems, especially among young married couples with small children. The divorce rate in America is over 50 percent. There can be little doubt that money issues are a big part of that extraordinary failure rate. When there isn't enough money, your choices are limited. It becomes a matter of paying monthly bills or doing fun things with the family, or buying new furniture, or purchasing a new car or nicer house, or going out to dinner and a movie, or going on vacation. In too many cases, we try to do all or many of these things even without enough money on hand. We use credit cards or borrow money to get and do the things we want, leading to more debt (often making just the minimum monthly payment required). The debt creates more fixed expenses and less discretionary money, so the cycle not only starts over, but also may get worse. As this downward spiral of debt spins more and more out of control, we may start arguing with our spouse or significant others, not be in the mood to do fun things with our mate or kids, and we won't have the money to do the things we would like with family and friends.

This can take a terrible toll on a relationship. It can lead to arguments and pressure for all adults in a household to work full-time outside the home, work over-time, even to take on a second job whether or not that was part of the original life plan. Children are left on their own more than is desirable, and the parents cannot participate in all their activities, which leads to more stress and probably more family turmoil. This kind of stress can even lead to sexual dysfunction for both men and women, further harming a marital relationship. We simply may be spending so much time working to make money and thinking about our money problems that we are rarely in the mood to do anything else. Again, the money problem downward spiral not only may continue, but also worsen over time. Sadly, this stress can result in abusive behavior (verbal, physical, psychological) of spouse and children. It also is often reported as a major cause of suicide.

However, it isn't just immediate family relationships that suffer. We may lack the time and financial ability to visit relatives and friends, participate in outings or trips, and even attend special events like weddings and graduation celebrations. We may end up growing more distant from these support groups, adding to our mental and physical stress and detracting from our enjoyment of life.

Getting a Job

It is hard to find a job with money problems: too little money or available credit limit to make sure you have a decent wardrobe, to pay for job interview trips until and if they are reimbursed, or to pay moving expenses until and if your new employer repays that expense. Even more troublesome is the fact that employers are increasingly using the credit scores of job applicants as a serious screening tool. This is done under the assumption that people with bad credit have demonstrated a lack of personal responsibility and are likely to be distracted from their work duties when thinking about money problems.

Work Performance

Money problems tend to become a downward money/stress cycle that gets progressively worse since it usually impacts how we perform at work, regardless of the type of job we have. And, of course, this is where all the parts of this negative problem may lead to disaster. We miss work, or under-perform at work due to stress-related problems. Our work suffers, and we may fail to get merit increases in salary, qualify for over-time opportunities, get passed up for a promotion, or lose our job due to poor performance. All of this, of course, can add dramatically to our stress, money problems, and relationships problems with family members. Furthermore, your chance of getting a different job opportunity diminishes significantly if you have a relatively poor record of performance on your current job.

Self-Esteem

Possibly the most overlooked result of this downward cycle is the negative impact on a person's self-esteem. This isn't just another problem in the money/stress cycle; it may be a devastating blow because it can affect your ability to recover from the problems mentioned earlier. If we think of ourselves as failures, that we can't manage our money, or earn enough to provide for our family, or simply to live the way we want, we may become depressed and feel hopeless. This also can affect the way we think others see us: as a financial failure or loser. Sadly, such self-perceptions, whether or not justified, may become a self-fulfilling prophecy.

Happiness

Ultimately, the cumulative negative impact of financial problems leads to unhappiness. We all remember learning in school about our founding fathers' desire to create a country in which we all have the right to "life, liberty and the pursuit of happiness." But we have to remember those last few words: that we don't have the right to happiness, simply the *pursuit* of it. It is up to us to achieve happiness in our lives. We need to learn to manage our life and money to achieve our goals. Financially, this means that we need to control our money and not let it control us!

However, you also have to remember that having all the money you need or want does not necessarily create happiness. There are too many stories of tragedy, sadness, and loneliness among the wealthy to think that you can achieve everything you want with monetary success alone. Once again, you need to focus on *whole life* management rather than just *personal financial* management. Finances are an important component that needs to be addressed in your planning, but it may not, by itself, create the happiness we desire in our lives. In this author's opinion, financial well-being is a *necessary, but not sufficient condition for happiness*.

Note

This last section on the "money problem" has been what my generation might call "a real downer," and it was supposed to be. Too many authors sugarcoat the negative aspects of failing at money management (or anything for that matter) in order not to disturb the reader too much. Well, you should be disturbed. Hopefully, disturbed into positive action.

---

4. Start Planning: The Prerequisites

The "Let's Be Honest" Part of Planning

Assessing your current behavior in personal financial planning may seem like an academic exercise (and, the fact that the author has confessed to being a college professor may offer a logical explanation to this approach). But be assured, this is a necessary and critical step in the slow and hard process of achieving your financial goals. You must take a long, hard, and methodical look at what you currently are doing, both right and wrong. Let's start with a personal quiz (after all, this wouldn't be a respectable self-help book without a quiz or two), but we aren't going to score it since **there are no right or wrong answers.**

I know, you think you are too young and have too little money or other assets to worry about this. WRONG! This is exactly the time to start thinking about money issues so that you won't have to worry about it as much when you're older. Remember, one of the biggest mistakes we make with money management is to wait until our 40s or 50s to really seriously think about it. While late is better than never, it is often too late at mid life to maximize what could have been a financially independent future, based on good money management and, just as importantly, good life management.

As noted earlier, the perfect time to have started money management is when you first received an allowance from your parents or started to receive monetary gifts from relatives. This is when your parents should have started you on the right path, financially speaking. Unfortunately, as also noted earlier, your parents, like most of us, weren't trained in this either and they were or are probably focused just on keeping their heads above these often turbulent financial waters. Even people who earn a good salary often have problems—usually the overspending type of problem—, but that is often just a symptom of poor life planning.

Quick-Fix Alert!

Whenever you see points used for scoring a quiz in a self-help book, run for the hills. This is a simple gimmick to make readers feel like this is a scientific analysis. We tend to find quantitative figures more believable, whether or not they are accurate. The real usefulness of such quizzes is to help readers assess their own behavior. The quizzes below allow you to carefully review your behavior within the context of your personal values and goals (and to make sure you have identified, in specific terms, those values and goals you have). This process is neither simple nor quick and does not provide a "scientific" answer.

Personal Finance Self-Assessment

Below, is a personal finance quiz that you should try to answer to the best of your ability and as honestly as possible. Unlike quizzes you may have had in school, there are no right or wrong answers here, but your responses may help you focus on many of the issues that will be discussed later in this book.

Figure 1: Personal Finance Quiz

1. Could you better manage the money you have? Yes ___, No___
2. Are you striving to do better financially? Yes ___, No___
3. Do you like to have every new technological gadget? Yes ___, No___
4. Do you always want the latest trendy clothes? Yes ___, No___
5. Do you want to make sure your children (if and when you have them) have a better life than you did growing up? Yes ___, No___
6. Do you want to be able to retire at the youngest age possible? Yes ___, No___
7. Do you have credit card debt carried over month to month? Yes ___, No___
8. Are you living at or below your means (can you pay all your bills every month, plus other monthly living expenses and debt payments and still have some left over)? Yes ___, No___
9. Is money always the primary factor in your consumer purchases? Yes ___, No___

10. Do you think you have enough savings to live for six months without a paycheck? Yes ___, No___
11. As of today, do you have retirement savings in an IRA, your employer's retirement plan, a 401k plan, etc.? Yes ___, No___
12. Do you maximize the amount of tax-deferred retirement savings you can afford to have taken out of your pay at work (the maximum that most of us can afford to save this way is between 15 and 20% of our gross income/month)? Yes ___, No___
13. How much do you save, on average, per month in addition to any tax-deferred retirement savings through your employer? $_____
14. How much discretionary spending do you have each month (after all regular bills and debt payments and planned savings)? $_____
15. How do you usually spend your discretionary money? (List the top five categories such as entertainment, etc.)?
    1. _____
    2. _____
    3. _____
    4. _____
    5. _____
16. How many credit cards do you have (and what are they: gas card, bankcards, store cards such as Macy's, Home Depot, etc.)? #___ Types_____
17. Approximately how much debt do you have right now?
    $_____ All credit cards?
    $_____ Installment loans (car, etc.)?
    $_____ College loans?
    $_____ Mortgage (balance/years left)?
    $_____ 2nd mortgage/home equity loans?
    $_____ Other?
18. What are your current assets? (check your records)
    $_____ Checking accounts?
    $_____ Savings accounts?
    $_____ Investments?
    $_____ Real estate (market value of any you own)?
    $_____ Major saleable personal property other than your house (art, antiques, jewelry, autos)?
19. Do you have a financial budget for monthly income and expenses? Yes___, No___
20. If you answered Yes in #19, do you record your expenditures and periodically compare it to your budget? Yes ___, No___

Your answers to the financial self-assessment questions should be both thought-provoking and eye-opening. Basically, your answers to these questions should help you assess: 1. how aware you are of your current financial situation (i.e., how hard it was to find the answer to some of the specific financial questions); 2. if you are satisfied with the financial part of your life; and 3. whether or not you are living above your means. Let's face it: most of us want to start out in life where our parents left off (to live the same as they do now at the time when we start our own household for the first time), and that just isn't realistic in most cases. Or, we may, in the classic sense, be trying to keep up with the Jones (our neighbors or friends). If we can't pay all of our bills every month, or after paying them, have too little left over to live the way we want, we not only become frustrated and probably stressed-out, but we also tend to go further in debt as a short-term solution to the immediate problem rather than trying to really fix it.

Have you ever questioned how important it really is to have new gadgets, the trendiest clothes, or the newest car? If these are important to you, do you have a plan to acquire them, or do you give in to the temptation for immediate gratification facilitated by easy access to credit? And, why do many of us want to make a better life for our kids than we had (unless we were actually deprived as children)? What's wrong with a good, loving childhood with all the basics provided and the luxuries being offered when we can afford them and choose to indulge ourselves? Let's face it: the only ones who really benefit when each succeeding generation tries to improve the material well-being of their offspring are the sellers of new goods and services and the financial institutions that help finance our apparently insatiable desire for material goods and consumer services before we have the money to pay for them in cash.

Many of the questions in the quiz above relate to factual financial information that we all should be able to answer. Your answers not only should help you determine if you have the necessary information to assess your financial position, but the specific data you need for the quiz, once obtained, also should give you a clear picture of where you're at right now financially. A few may be pleased, but many readers will be shocked at how precarious their financial position really is or how little attention they pay to it. Anyone who can answer all of the questions without looking up information may be what young people refer to as "anal." However, the people who can't answer these questions without a major research effort are what financial planners would call "dangerously uninformed"—in danger, regardless of income level, of financial crisis due to inattention to their financial position. People who aren't well aware of their financial position are probably the ones who do not have clear financial goals; yet, having clear goals is the first prerequisite stage of financial planning. Some reports regarding Gen Y suggest that many members of your generation are financially illiterate (though this author thinks that may apply to several other generations as well). [13] In any case, let's make sure "they" are wrong, at least about you; by the time you finish this book you should have clear financial goals, an overall financial plan, and a current budget to follow.

5. Determining Your Life Targets
A Prerequisite to Integrating Life and Financial Planning

People who have no plan for their financial well-being are not very likely to have a general life plan either. However, many people who have some semblance of a financial plan also may not have a life plan. Quite honestly, it is impossible to have a useful financial plan unless we know what we want out of life. A stand-alone financial plan simply is incomplete unless we know what else is important in our lives and how that finance plan fits into the whole picture (once again, that "holistic" planning issue that was mentioned earlier). In other words, financial goals do not mean much if we don't have clear life goals. Our motivation to follow a financial plan without clear life goals is likely to be very low, ultimately leading to plan failure.

The values and goals exercise below (see Figure 2) is designed to get you to think about your general values and goals and to encourage you to state them as clearly and explicitly as possible. Once again, there are no right or wrong answers to this quiz, and no points to quickly score your "life goals aptitude" or some other self-help gimmick. The only requirement is that you try to answer the questions as honestly as possible. Again, this isn't a quick fix approach. Rather, it is a "hard-work method" that may require a great deal of introspection and discussion with your most significant others. And remember, this isn't a class, so take as much time as needed to answer the questions. (See Appendix 2: Hints for Developing Values and Goals)

Values and Goals Assessment

For most of you, this exercise probably will require a great deal of time and effort, and possibly frustration. But the time and effort you expend trying to answer these questions may be the most important single thing you can do not only to better plan your finances, but also to plan for the life you desire.

Figure 2: General Values and Life Goals Exercise

1. What are your most important *personal values*; i.e., what is most important to you in life? If you don't know or are not sure, then you really need to take some time to think about this. Take a look at the list below and (1) check any that you think are, in fact, important values to you, and (2) add any other values that are important but not listed. (Remember, values are very broad, sort of your personal "mission statement" in life.)

    ___ Happy/stable family life
    ___ Good health
    ___ Personal happiness
    ___ Good friendships
    ___ Faith/religion
    ___ Helping others
    ___ Meaningful career/professional recognition
    ___ Wealth accumulation
    ___ Personal freedom
    ___ Patriotism
    Other (list below):

    ___ _____
    ___ _____
    ___ _____
    ___ _____

2. Now, for all the values you checked (and/or added) in #1 above, try to *prioritize those values*. In other words, which values are most important? Place a number next to the goals you checked (with 1= top priority; 2 = next highest; and so on).
    ___ Happy/stable family life
    ___ Good health
    ___ Personal happiness
    ___ Good friendships
    ___ Faith/religion
    ___ Helping others
    ___ Meaningful career/professional recognition
    ___ Wealth accumulation
    ___ Freedom to "do what you want, when you want"
    ___ Patriotism
    Other (list below):

    ___ _____
    ___ _____
    ___ _____
    ___ _____

3. What specific goals do you have to achieve to conform to the values you identified?

    - *Non-financial goals* (For example: if one of your values is family life, you may have a goal such as: "I hope to get married and have children.")

        (1) _____
        (2) _____
        (3) _____
        (4) _____
        (5) _____

    - *Financial goals* (For example: If one of your values is personal freedom, you may have a goal such as: "to have enough saved to retire by age 55.")

        (1) _____
        (2) _____
        (3) _____
        (4) _____
        (5) _____

4. What is the *time frame* for each of the goals you stated?
    N = Near-Term (to be achieved within the next five years)
    L = Long-Term (to be achieved within the next ten years)
    VLT = Very Long-Term (to be achieved before you retire)
    LA = Life Achievement (to be achieved during your life)

5. Are your goals consistent (e.g., Are your near-term goals going to help achieve your long-term goals, and will those goals help achieve your very long-term and life achievement goals?)? If not, revise your goals to make them consistent.

6. Do your goals meet the following criteria?

    - Are your goals achievable (realistic)? If not, revise them.
    - Are your goals specific and measureable? They need to be in order to evaluate your achievements.

7. And the BIG QUESTION: Do you have a *specific plan of action* to achieve your near-term goals? (**Note:** This is the point where many plans fail. Even large organizations involved in "strategic planning" often fail to fully understand the importance of putting their stated goals into action, somehow thinking that just having goals is a good enough guide to decision-making.)

    - Do you have objectives for the coming year in order to begin meeting your highest priority near-term goals?
    - What specific steps or actions are you going to take to implement your plan?
    - What is your timetable to implement each action in the upcoming year?
    - Are these steps written down?

Note

> As a practical matter, we should be putting our greatest effort towards achieving goals and objectives that relate to our highest priority values. A mistake many people make is to try to accomplish everything at once, which often leads to not accomplishing anything completely or well.

The results of this exercise should not be looked at as written in stone. There is no rule saying that you can't change your goals (though we tend to maintain our basic values for a longer period of time, often for a lifetime). In fact, our goals are likely to change as we get older. At 20, we may think we have a good shot at being a CEO of a large corporation. At 50 we may realize that we have not done what it is going to take to achieve that goal, or, just as likely, that we really don't want that position and all that goes with it.

The sheer number of goals that we identify may be of concern. For those who could only come up with one or two, you need to spend much more time contemplating your life and what you want from it. For most people, however, the problem will have been the excessive number of goals identified, so many that it would be unlikely, if not impossible, to achieve them all. Thus, the need to prioritize your goals, which simply means deciding what is most important to you. Successful people (people who are fully satisfied with their life and what they have accomplished) tend to have been very focused on a few important goals. When trying to accomplish too many goals, we tend to spread ourselves too thin and often end up not doing anything very well or finding that we have accomplished less important goals that were more easily attained and failed to attain our higher-level goals. For example, financial goals might be pursued by taking the best paying employment position you can find, but a goal of being happy and feeling a sense of accomplishment (assuming the latter is a higher level goal for most people) may be sacrificed.

If, in the process of completing the above exercise you find that your goals are, in fact, not consistent, that you have too many, or that your goals do not meet the basic criteria for effective goals, then you should revise and restate them. It is important to remember that there is no right or wrong set of goals, in spite of what your family, friends and co-workers might think if you divulged your goals to them. It is only important that you and your most significant others agree. I'm not even convinced that your children, if and when you have them, should be consulted, since, with luck, they will be on their own by their early 20s and have to go through this process for themselves.

A sad fact of life is that many of us spend far too much time trying to please others, to achieve goals they think we should have (typically reflecting their own). Though probably well intentioned, it is unfair to superimpose your goals on others, even people close to you (and they should refrain from doing so as well). That said, in order for you to manage your finances, you must clearly understand what your financial goals are and where they stand relative to your other life goals; specifically, what priority you place on financial goals relative to other goals. The latter is essential if you are to have a meaningful plan for managing your money. It can only be done effectively if it is done in the context of a whole life plan, once again reinforcing the importance of taking a "holistic" approach to financial planning.

6. Developing Your Life Plan

The not-so-well kept secret to success in most areas of life is the need for well thought out and executed plans. With a good plan, you can achieve almost anything you are capable of doing. Without a specific plan of action based on concrete goals and objectives, you are just daydreaming. Sure, we have to account for natural talent and intellect, but most of us probably never come close to what we could achieve in all facets of our lives simply because, unlike the Nike slogan, we just "don't do it." We fail to do most things that we want to do simply because we don't have a good plan of action, based on realistic and measurable goals.

As you read this section of the book, you may be wondering what the heck topics such as stress management, time management, organizing your physical environment, health, fitness, appearance, as well as interpersonal relationships have to do with financial planning—probably even questioning whether the author is taking this holistic planning thing too far. Well, to some extent that may be true. At the same time, it is important to remember that all of the life plan topics have a potential impact on your finances and, conversely, are likely to be affected by your financial position/capability.

It makes sense that people who cannot manage these important parts of their life are not likely to be motivated or capable of planning finances. Consequently, we need to take the old adage "love thyself" to a higher level. That is, not only love thyself, but also work to develop a life-long plan to achieve all that you want to accomplish in the short time we mortals have on earth.

As with most things that are important to us, a good life plan is not easily achieved. An effective plan requires not only hard work, but also a plan of action. You must have specific objectives for each part of the plan with a timetable to both start and accomplish those objectives. You must then determine the specific course(s) of action to take to implement the plan. Of course, great care must be taken in the implementation stage since that is where many plans become unrealized good intentions. Finally, you have to determine if you can do this on your own, with the aid of "self-help" guides, or if you need professional assistance.

Disclaimer

Certainly, for some of the topics in this section, you may want to consult other authors in order to get another point of view. What is offered here are some basic ideas to consider, starting with the need for a personal life plan.

However, remember the "quick-fix" warning for all self-help sources (including the book you are reading): they should be read with caution, particularly those that suggest a quick or easy solution (which definitely does not include this book). In other words, rely on your instincts and common sense to sort out good advice from the mass of ineffectual ideas that plague this genre of books.

It also should be noted that, for those who are married or have a significant other, it is appropriate to develop an "us" life plan as well as, but not in lieu of, a "me" plan. It will be easier to achieve your desired goals if you coordinate your efforts with other people who are important in your life, particularly a spouse or significant other. If you are in a long-term relationship, a life plan that only focuses on you may be doomed from the start. Conversely, if you don't feel the need to consult the person with whom you have a relationship, maybe the latter is not all that it could or should be.

Managing Stress

The Benefits of Managing Stress

Managing your stress effectively can dramatically improve your life. Stress affects all of us, albeit at different levels, and impacts many facets of life. Stress can significantly affect our physical and mental health (it actually can contribute to death), but it also can seriously impact personal relationships with family and friends, job performance, ability to relax (personal happiness), and might even affect our looks ("stress lines" on some people's faces). In addition, because of its pervasive impact on your life, it can potentially have serious financial consequences.

Why It's a Problem

Unfortunately, stress is an area where you might run into a serious "catch 22": stress can have all of the negative impacts on your life noted above, but all those same factors (money problems, relationship issues, job pressures, health problems) often are the major contributors to that increased stress.

U.S. workers are frequently cited as being among the most stressed-out workers in industrialized countries, citing financial concerns as the primary cause of their stress. [4] Europeans often note that, while they "work to live," Americans seem to "live to work." Certainly the Judeo-Christian work ethic does still exist, with such accompanying clichés as "work hard, live well," or "idle hands are the devil's workshop." But it is much more complicated than just being a characteristic of U.S. culture. Most Americans are admittedly hedonistic and materialistic. We are pleasure seekers, and we usually want immediate gratification of our desires and perceived needs. We tend to want to live as well as we can in terms of our possessions: having a fancy car, big house, all the newest communication and entertainment technology, etc. And we want it all now, rather than later. Gen Y has not been immune to this trend. Some would say that it has increased (worsened?) with each generation. However, with middle class "real" income stagnating over the last 20-25 years (income adjusted for changes in the cost of goods and services), our wants and perceived needs often are not matched by our income, thus increasing stress, which is then further increased if we use debt to finance those things we can't afford with our current income. [2] If we start using debt to support our desired lifestyle, that increasing debt load ultimately will impede our ability to buy more of the goods and services we want, as well as our ability to save for future needs including retirement.

Gen Y is also much more subject to stress resulting from visual and audio overload than previous generations. You not only have TV and radio, along with newspapers, magazines and books as did previous generations, but you also have access to cable TV with an expansive array of stations as well as pay-per-view options. You have DVD players and DVRs to tape multiple programs while you watch another or do some other activity. You have laptop, notebook and tablet computers with Wi-Fi, along with your smart phones to not only stay in frequent contact with close friends and family via calls, text or email, but also to access easily the Internet and the rapidly increasing number of social media sites, which allow many young people to develop an ever expanding world of cyber friends. This overload can affect work as well as social life, making both more efficient, but also create a great deal more stress for having to stay connected 24/7 with friends and employers. New technologies certainly make life more interesting and allow more connectivity between people close or far away. But, all new technologies also have a downside, not the least of which is stress.

The Process

The first thing we need to do in order to reduce stress is to assess what is causing that stress in your life. What is making you happy/excited/satisfied in life (positives)? Conversely, what in your life is making you unhappy/anxious/angry (negatives)? In addition, what are the parts of your life that make you neither happy nor unhappy; they are just unavoidable parts of your life (neutrals)?

TABLE 1-a: STRESS SELF-ASSESSMENT

POSITIVES Things/activities that make me happy, excited or satisfied.	NEGATIVES Things/activities that make me angry, anxious, unhappy, etc.	NEUTRALS Things/activities that don't make me happy or unhappy.
1.	1.	1.
2.	2.	2.
3.	3.	3.
4.	4.	4.
5.	5.	5.
Etc.	Etc.	Etc.

After completing this self-assessment (even if that is just listing items/category), you should determine *how important* each of the things/activities you listed is in your personal and work life (important in terms of your goals and objectives). You should then go to the Stress Self-Assessment Table 1-b below and indicate for each thing/activity in all three columns in Table 1-a the **priority** you attach for each activity you listed (**1**= High; **2** = Medium; **3** = Low).

ALERT!

You already may have figured out that there are a number of these self-assessment quizzes in this book. Again, there are no right or wrong answers, but the more seriously you take these exercises, the better you will be able to develop a complete life plan that works for you.

When you review this stress assessment, it should give you an idea of the things and activities you feel are both positive and highly important, positive with medium importance, etc. However, it also should help determine what actions to take to deal with both the positive and negative things going on in your life, as well as those you consider to be neutral. For example, those things/activities that are neutral and less important may be able to be ignored or at least put off until more important, less stressful things in your life have been completed. Depending on how confident you are in your assessment, the following guideline might be useful in managing your stress.

TABLE 1-b: STRESS SELF-ASSESSMENT AND ACTIONS

SELF-ASSESSMENT	SUGGESTED ACTION
Positives/High Priority 1. 2. 3.	A stress reducing **no-brainer**. Something you should or have to do, but also makes you happy/excited.
Positives/Medium Priority 1. 2. 3.	Also a stress reducer. You should try to find a way to **do this activity when possible.**
Positives/Low Priority 1. 2. 3.	This is something that could be **postponed** until higher priorities have been satisfied.

Negatives/High Priority 1. 2. 3.	**Just get it done.** If possible, delegate this to someone else; possibly pay someone to do it.
Negatives/Medium Priority 1. 2. 3.	This could be **postponed** until higher priority "must-do" activities are completed (and also is a candidate for delegation to someone else).
Negatives/Low Priority 1. 2. 3.	**Reduce stress by avoiding this activity!**
Neutrals/High Priority 1. 2. 3.	This activity is a **"non-stress causing must do,"** so include it in your schedule.
Neutrals/Medium Priority 1. 2. 3.	This is an activity that might **also be delegated or put off until higher priority activities are completed.**
Neutrals/Low Priority 1. 2. 3.	**"Planned procrastination."** Put these activities off until you have other tasks completed.

The self-assessment does not tell you what to do, but should provide a framework for you to begin planning how you can reduce/minimize the stress in your life and better understand the stress that cannot be eliminated but possibly better controlled. If we don't manage our stress-related activities relative to our life plan priorities, we may find ourselves focusing on things/activities that make us happy or feel good, but that may not be as important as other activities in the total scheme of things in our life. And this WILL lead to an increase in stress!

Hints to Reduce Stress

- **First and foremost, actually complete the previous self-assessment exercise** in order to develop a plan to set priorities based on a review of your goals and objectives. The plan should help to significantly reduce stress; the exercise should help you get a clear picture of what has been causing your stress and where you can change your behavior to best reduce or eliminate that stress.

- All the other subjects in this book relate to stress (thus, possible stress reducers).
  - **Organize your physical environment at home and work.** As per the previous discussion, this relates closely to time management. Being organized reduces stress that can build up in your everyday life. Just knowing where your things are when you want them at any given time reduces anxiety and stress in your life as well as in the lives of those around you.
  - **Managing your time well.** This is one of the best ways to minimize stress. Remember that you probably can't do it all. There are only 168 hours in each and every week of the year, so you need to manage your time to accomplish your prioritized goals and objectives (time management is the topic of the next section of the book).
  - **Develop and maintain close friendships.** It was already noted that stress can impact personal relationships, but medical experts and psychologists also have documented that having frequent interaction with close friends reduces stress (and actually seems to extend our less stressful lives). So make an effort to develop friendships with those around you with whom you have things in common or just seem to connect. But don't forget old friends. Many adult men, and some (but fewer) women let old friendships slip away over time for a variety of reasons and focus instead on family, coworkers, and neighbors, which are important relationships but never quite the same as old friends from school and early adulthood. So for Gen Y and Z, don't let this happen if you can help it. And with modern communication technology, there is no good reason not to stay in touch with close friends even if they live far away.
  - **Establish a clear professional/career development plan.** Having a direction in life is a stress reducer, even if that direction changes over time. For example, if you need more education or training to move in a desired career direction, then start planning how you actually can get that training. Furthering your education/training can cause stress in your work and

family life, but it is a good (or acceptable) kind of stress; the kind that helps you accomplish something that will improve your life and your family's life.

o **Personal development activities are also stress reducers**. Doing things that make you feel better about yourself (e.g., weight loss, exercising, better grooming and hygiene, new clothes, etc.) can help you reduce your psychologically-based stress. This can make you feel more confident in your interpersonal relationships at both work and play, which, of course, will also help reduce stress. In fact, some activities such as exercise and weight loss actually can reduce medical/health-related stress problems such as hypertension.

o **Financial planning can be a major stress reducer** (see the "personal finance connection" below).

Note

This may be a good time to point out that there is both good and bad stress. Some amount of real or anticipated stress may provide stimulation in your work and may make you more careful in other activities such as driving, paying attention to directions or instructions from your superiors, or remembering important dates pertaining to either family or work. Good types of stress can push you to perform activities more carefully and with better results.

Bad stress is destructive. It is the kind of stress that leads you to be over-anxious rather than appropriately anxious when performing a new task. It might lead you to avoid activities that need to be done. It may be a result of obsessing over your behavior or performance, particularly when you know that you could have done better and that most of the fault for not doing better was beyond your immediate control. You get the idea!

- *Some miscellaneous ideas for stress reduction:*

  o Take the vacation time your employer gives you (or, if self employed, take some time off). Americans take fewer and shorter vacations than almost any other advanced industrial society. And, when you go on vacation (even if it's a so-called "stay-cation"), you should try to disconnect technologically from work and other non-personal commitments. Maybe you can't bear to leave the cell phone, tablet, laptop, etc. at home, but turn them off and don't answer anything other than an emergency call, text or email.

o Get enough sleep. Most studies show that people who get 7-9 hours of uninterrupted sleep appear to have less stress or are better equipped to handle the inevitable stress that occurs in everyone's life. Of course this is another "catch-22" in life, since stress also can lead to difficulty sleeping.

o Learn to use "waiting time" productively. Whether waiting in a doctor's office, for a plane, stuck in traffic, etc., there is always something we can do that is useful either to work or just doing something we like to do, *if* we are prepared. You will be less frustrated at the wait time, and, therefore, less stressed. For example:

  ▪ Have a book/E-book with you to read (something we often have difficulty finding time to do).

  ▪ Write text messages or emails or make a phone call that you have put off because you didn't have time.

  ▪ Have your personal planner with you because it might need updating.

• **Consider seeking professional help**. If you have a significant amount of stress in your life, including symptoms of hard-to-control anger which is often related to high levels of stress in a person's life, you should not hesitate to see a psychologist* who specializes in stress or anger management. Or you could consult with medical professionals, though I personally believe that it is better to see a psychologist first since they will not default to medications as some medical professionals might do. Furthermore, most well qualified psychologists would not hesitate to refer you to a medical professional if they thought it was a condition that might require medication.

---

*Note

For those who may not know the difference, most psychologists or psychological therapists are not medical doctors (they would have a Master's degree or Ph.D. in psychology), whereas a psychiatrist is a medical doctor who completed a specialty in psychiatric medicine.

The "Personal Finance" Connection

Stress can and often does lead to serious financial problems. It can contribute significantly to physical and emotional health problems. Individuals suffering from stress often incur significant costs. For example: increased health care costs, lost promotions or, worse, lost jobs, and difficulty with interpersonal relationships (stress has been determined to be a major contributing factor in divorce). All of these consequences can have a significant financial cost, which is likely to exacerbate stress, ultimately turning into a major ongoing cycle of stress, personal problems, financial distress, and more stress. This cycle not only can lead to destroyed relationships and careers, but also to financial calamity.

At the same time, financial problems are often one of the biggest problems in people's lives. Worrying about money issues causes significant stress not just to you, but also to your significant others/family and to everyone else around you. Many family arguments are about money: that you don't make enough to live the way you want to live; that you spend too much on things; that you aren't saving enough for major purchases (house, car, vacations, education, etc.); that you don't have a safety net for unanticipated events that could have a serious financial impact; or that you haven't saved for retirement. Managing your finances well can reduce much of this stress.

Clearly, personal financial planning and stress are interrelated parts of a whole life plan. In fact, stress can be related to every one of the life skills mentioned in this book, as well as to financial well-being, reinforcing the need to look at life planning as a holistic project.

Managing Time

The Benefits of Time Management

Time is finite, so you really need to develop a plan for efficient use of time. Time management affects, or is affected by, every other facet of your life plan. If you organize yourself and your physical environment, one of the major benefits will be additional time to spend on other activities that are important to you. We also know poor management of time can be a major cause of stress in your life, affecting both your personal and social relationships as well as your job performance—the life balance you maintain between work, home, and play. And, as the old saying goes "time is money;" specifically, wasted time may result in a loss of money, or at least a loss of opportunity to make money.

Efficient use of time simply allows you to get more done, to better meet your life goals and current objectives. Better use of time usually leads to better job performance, more quality time with family, friends and significant others, as well as more "alone time" (which will become more and more precious the older you get). As noted earlier, a more efficient use of time will, in almost all cases, reduce your stress with all the benefits that often accompany that achievement.

Why It's a Problem

Time is a cultural concept as well as a fixed unit of measurement. In the U.S., we focus on the fixed nature of time. There is only so much of it: 168 hours a week, 52 weeks/year, etc. In our culture, we see time more as a commodity than a concept. We attribute a waste of time to laziness and irresponsibility. Wasted time may result in lost opportunities for making money as well as pursuing your desired career or personal relationships; generally, achieving your other life goals. Moreover, unlike real commodities, once lost, time cannot be recaptured, at least not in our current understanding of physics.

Another problem is that use of time is not totally discretionary (and the older you get, at least until retirement, the less discretionary it seems to be). Certainly you have to sleep and spend some time on other normal, societal requisites such as personal hygiene. Plus, you have to eat, and that takes time even if you are a "microwave-only" cook. You also will have some commute time to consider unless you work from home. If you have an employer, you are highly likely to have expected work hours, as well as after-work responsibilities in many jobs.

To successfully avoid many of the problems with poor use of time and to gain the benefits of efficient use of time, you need to develop a plan to manage your time.

The Process

As noted above, time has a fixed limit, thus allowing (or requiring, you can choose which term you prefer) the use of one of most planners' favorite tools—a budget! However, the first step in the process is to record your current use of time, assess that use of time, and then create a time budget that is both **realistic** and **flexible**—both of which are absolute requirements for a successful budget of any kind.

Record Your Normal Use of Time
You need to accurately record your use of time over several "average" weeks; ones with no holidays or special events in your life such as weddings to attend, other celebrations, business trips, vacations, etc., in order to have as accurate a picture as possible of your typical use of time per day and per week. This step is tedious and time-consuming, but absolutely necessary—so just do it!

Note

This step is for your eyes only, so it needs to be as accurate and honest as possible. This is NOT a picture of how you would like to be spending your time (that will come later). It is meant to be a picture of how you actually use your time.

Use a daily time grid: a 24-hour grid broken down into 1 or ½-hour slots. (See Appendix 3: Sample Time Plan). Record your activities by specific category every day (Monday through Sunday) for three weeks (non-consecutive weeks if possible). Develop your own list of categories with reasonable specificity, such as:

1. Sleep
2. Eating
3. Personal hygiene
4. Commuting time
5. Work
6. Time with significant other/family
7. Time with friends
8. Leisure/Recreation/Sports
9. Home chores (yard/house etc.)
10. Shopping
11. Free time (no commitments)
12. Other

Assess Your Use of Time

After you record your actual use of time, you need to **assess** the time you normally spend on the various activities you are engaged in. In order to do this, you also need to review your stated goals and short-term objectives and prioritize the activities you have listed in your record of time use (as a High, Medium, or Low priority). From a review of the record you developed on time spent, you need to assess whether you are currently spending too much, just enough, or too little time on each of your designated activities.

TABLE 2: TIME MANAGENET SELF-ASSESSMENT TABLE
(Sample)

Categories of activities listed in your record of how time is used. For example:	Priority based on review of goals and objectives: **High, Medium,** or **Low**. For example:	Assess time spent / activity: too much; just enough; too little time. For example:
1. Sleep	1. High	1. Too little
2. Eating	2. Low	2. Just enough
3. Personal hygiene	3. High	3. Just enough
4. Commuting	4. Medium	4. Too much
5. Working	5. High	5. Just enough
6. Time with family	6. High	6. Too little
7. Time with friends	7. Medium	7. Too little
8. Etc.	8. Etc.	8. Etc.

This assessment should help determine your desired balance between work, home, leisure, etc. In many cases you may find out you are trying to do it all but just don't have enough time to do it all well! Sorry to tell you, but apart from the unrealistic drivel offered in many self-help books and seminars, most humans cannot do everything they would like to do or feel they should do unless they are retired/unemployed, without a significant other or dependents, and have very modest goals in life. However, it is also true that there are just some things we have to do, like it or not (sleeping and eating come to mind), but we can usually find ways to minimize (or maybe eliminate) the time we spend on less important activities.

Develop Your Time Budget

Develop a new daily time grid (a 24-hour grid broken down into 1 or ½-hour slots; again, see Appendix 3 for a sample time budget). Based on the prioritization of activities (above) that you did after reviewing your goals and objectives, you are now ready to create a desired time schedule that reflects a more appropriate budgeting of your limited time. Start by looking at your original record of time use and do the following, based on your prioritization:

- Add more time to any high priority activities for which you were not previously allowing enough time.
- Reduce the time for high priority activities for which you might have been allocating too much time.
- Then, add or reduce time for medium priority activities based on your earlier assessment.
- For low priority activities, either:
  o eliminate these activities from your schedule if possible;
  o reduce the time allotted for these activities; or
  o reallocate these activities to less "prime" times.
- Make sure your time budget has allowed for adequate **free time** (time for which you have no prior commitments) that can be used either for additional relaxation in your busy life or, more importantly, as **flex time**: time that can be allocated for unanticipated activities that come up and which you feel you have to or want to do.

Implement Your Time Budget

Follow your time plan for several weeks—another "just do it" situation. After several weeks, evaluate the plan to see how it has worked, and, if necessary, modify and retry the plan for another couple weeks (time budgets often need some tweaking). Have contingency time plans for summer/holidays, emergencies, and other unanticipated events. But make a point of returning to your time plan as soon as possible. The more it becomes a habit, the better. Periodically review your time budget, even if it has been working well for you (things in your life change over time and your budget may need to be revised accordingly). Ultimately, the most important part of implementing any plan, including a time plan, is **YOU**. If you don't make a conscientious effort to follow your time plan, I can almost guarantee it won't work.

Hints to Consider

- **Routine is your friend!** Most young people hate routine; they find it unexciting, if not just boring. But routines save time and help prevent forgetting important tasks or becoming overwhelmed with the number of tasks to complete. Most of us leave for work the same time each day so that we get there on time, hopefully giving us a little leeway in case of unanticipated events, such as traffic problems, etc. The same concept can help you use your limited time well on other regular activities. For example:
  - Grocery shop the same day and time each week or bi-weekly, however that works best for your schedule.
  - Do your laundry the same time and day each week, so it becomes a habit and you always have clean clothes.
  - Have meals at the same time as much as possible on days you work outside of your home. That keeps your time plan more intact and better ensures that you eat regularly, which is important for energy to do work as well as good advice for better health and weight control. You can be more flexible on days off from work
  - You get the idea. Apply this to other regular activities where possible.
- **Procrastination is your enemy!** Most of us know instinctively that procrastination is not a good

characteristic. It often ruins otherwise good time schedules and is something that often leads to increased stress. Contrary to popular myth, we usually do not do things better when we have put them off until the last minute and have to get them done. In fact we usually either don't get the activity done or not done as well as it could have been had we had more time. Procrastination is a common practice in most people's busy lives, but it needs to be minimized if you want to accomplish your life goals, including your finances. Having a well thought out, flexible time plan with adequate free time (and time for unanticipated events) included can be helpful to significantly reduce a tendency towards procrastination, but only if you diligently follow that plan!

- **A "to do" list is a necessity.** This should be a daily/weekly/and probably monthly list of things you need to do, listed in a rank order of priority (i.e., what is most important to do first, and so on), and it should not be more extensive than what you can possibly get done in those time frames (some things just may have to wait for a future list). In addition to helping use your time effectively, this also helps to keep your life better organized. Just creating and having such a list and being able to cross off tasks accomplished can be a morale booster and stress reducer.
- **Avoid "time wasters."** Be aware of and try to minimize possible "time wasters" such as: TV watching, playing video games, talking or texting on your phone, and excessive use of social media such as Facebook, Twitter, etc. (92% of your generation use social media). [11]
- **Find "new time."** There may be times of day that you aren't using as well as you could. For example: (1) using lunch time to get work done; (2) using mass transit or car pooling to reduce stress and transportation costs as well as provide additional time to read emails, the newspaper, reports, etc.; (3) if sleeping more than 8 hours, getting up ½ hour earlier or going to bed ½ hour later; and (4) working smarter, getting more done in less time (avoiding distractions and interruptions).

The "Personal Finance" Connection

Once again, remember that time *is* money. Not only does efficient and effective use of time affect almost every part of your life, but it also can profoundly impact your finances in terms of, for example: devoting enough time to your job to maximize current and future compensation, having time to think about and anticipate personal needs so you can shop smartly for bargains, to allocate time for reviewing your financial situation (budgets/investments/debt payment/spending patterns/etc.) in order to better manage your finances. Effective time management also may help you identify time-consuming activities that might best be delegated so that you can spend more time on other things that will save you proportionately more money, or to make more money (work more hours), or better meet other life goals. In the second major section of this book, which focuses on financial planning, you will see additional time use implications.

Career and Professional Development

The Benefits of Developing a Career Plan

Earlier in this book, the alternative post-high school education/training options that are available to you were pointed out. It was also suggested that your choice could, and probably should, have been based on what kind of job/career or further education you were hoping to pursue. Yet, it's highly probable that many, if not most of you had at age 17, 18, or 19 no clear idea of exactly what job you might like and for which you had the appropriate talent or skills. Thus, you may have made no conscious choice; your parents, and you by default, just assumed you would or would not go to college. You may have selected a path that you seemed to like (or your friends or family recommended), or the one where you thought you could make the most money, etc. Fortunately, whatever choice you made in your late teens, 20s, or even 30s can be changed or modified.

You can change careers, move your current career in a different, but related direction, or just improve your skills for your current job to enhance your opportunity for promotion. More importantly, you don't have to quit your current job for many professional/career development opportunities, since these programs (both degree and non-degree certificate programs) are frequently offered online, or, conveniently, in local community colleges and sometimes in commercial venues or shopping centers in or near large metropolitan areas. Some employers may even offer in-house professional development. For those of you who are unhappy with your current job, there are many ways to alter your career path if you develop a clear and doable professional/career plan.

Why It's a Problem

Even if you consciously considered what type of post-high school education/training to purse, you may not have been able to connect the dots between that and a type of job or career consistent with each education/training option. Moreover, in many secondary schools in the U.S., the availability and quality of career counseling is not what it should or could be. While most colleges have a career service center, many tend to focus on post-graduation employment more than helping young people find the career path that may best suit them.

For a host of reasons, not the least of which is youth, we often make our post high-school education/training decisions prior to having a clear idea of what occupation we would like and for which we have the best raw skills or talent. This is why many college administrators, among others, suggest that college is more about learning how to learn, or learning for the sake of learning, rather than to train for a specific career. However, if you talk to admissions officers for colleges and universities, most will tell you that parents of prospective students ask more about the careers college education can lead to than almost any other issue (though the prospective students are often more concerned about the quality of the food service, dorm room amenities, and the recreation center). In fact, some colleges are starting to offer tuition discounts for students majoring in STEM (science, technology, engineering, and mathematics), what they deem the "most useful" majors, in order to encourage student selection of these fields of study. However, to do so just for a tuition discount may lead you into a career that you don't particularly like or for which you are not well suited. Of course some students, probably with the encouragement of their parents, are choosing majors based on starting salaries.

Two-year colleges and vocational/technical school programs are more directly career oriented. But, once again, those who attended those schools may have chosen this type of post-secondary education/training prior to determining their desired career area, and thus ended up simply choosing among the alternative career tracks offered rather than having thoroughly investigated what career or job might best suit them.

The Process

One of the first steps in the process of developing a career/professional plan is to determine what your career goals are; generally, do you live to work (is work the most important and satisfying part of your life?), or do you work in order to live the way you want? Not a bad question to answer if you do so honestly, but not specific enough for your planning purpose. You need to think through a number of issues in order to establish career goals that are a prerequisite to developing a career plan (see Figure 3).

Develop a Career or Job Plan

If you already have a clear and specific career or job plan, and are successfully accomplishing your career goals and objectives according to your timetable, good for you! However, it still might be a good idea to review and assess your current plan along the same lines suggested below for those who need to develop such a plan.

For those of you who do not have a current career plan, you need to do an assessment based on the quiz in Figure 3 below to start developing a plan to either find a new job or advance in your current position. You should, by this point in life, have a clear and specific set of career/job goals and objectives for the short term, near term, and long term and have a pretty good idea of whether or not your current job is meeting your career goals; thus whether your plan is to pursue a new career or to improve advancement opportunities in your current position. For those who would like to pursue a new career, you should also by now have considered what career/jobs might best meet your needs and desires. If not, go to Figure 4: Your Career or Job Plan and investigate other jobs that might better meet both your goals and skills. You should consider consulting the following website when trying to determine what career best suits you: **https://cdc-tree.stanford.edu/**

Figure 3: The Job and Career Planning Quiz

1. Do you currently have a specific career plan? Yes___, No___
   - If Yes:
     o Are you on track according to that plan? Yes ___, No___
     o Does that plan reflect your career and life goals? Yes___, No___
     o If yes:
       a. You should have specified short-term objectives (1 year), near-term goals (2-5 years) and long-term career goals (over 5 years, up to retirement). If not, you should do so; for example, your planned progression by type of job, rank, employer, etc.
       b. You should periodically review both your goals and your plan to see how well you are succeeding.
       c. Consider changes that might be needed in your career goals or plan as your life situation changes (getting married/divorced, having children, etc.).
   - If No:
     o What are your career goals?
       ___ To contribute to society.
       ___ To make money.
       ___ To become wealthy.
       ___ To provide a good life for my family and me.
       ___ To help people.
       ___ To achieve status and respect (beyond monetary success).
       ___ To enjoy what you do (actually want to go to work).
       ___ To be self-employed (no boss to report to).
       ___ Other (list):

       _____
       _____
       _____

     o If you have more than one career goal, go back and assign a priority to each one (e.g., high, medium, or low priority).
     o How does your current job measure up to your goals?
       ___ It currently meets all my goals.
       ___ I feel on track to meet my goals.
       ___ It only meets some of my goals.
       ___ It meets few if any of my goals.

2. What are your particular skills or talents?
   ___ Good people skills—you like interacting with others.
   ___ A willing and demonstrated leader—you like being in charge of projects/activities.
   ___ Good communication skills:
       ___ written communication
       ___ oral communication
       ___ listening/easily grasping ideas
   ___ Good quantitative skills

___ Good computer skills
    ___ basic skills (word processing, graphics, spread sheets, etc.)
    ___ advanced (describe: _____)
___ Good organization skills (able to multitask)
___ Creativity skills: e.g., arts, writing, acting, thinking, idea generation (specify):

_____
_____

___ Other (specify):

_____
_____

3.   Which of the talents and skills you listed above are used on your current job, and how well are they used (minimal to maximum use)?
    ___ Good people skills—you like interacting with others.
    ___ A willing and demonstrated leader—you like being in charge of projects/activities.
    ___ Good communication skills:
        ___ written communication
        ___ oral communication
        ___ listening/easily grasping ideas
    ___ Good quantitative skills
    ___ Good computer skills
        ___ basic skills (word processing, graphics, spread sheets, etc.)
        ___ advanced (describe: _____)
    ___ Good organization skills (able to multitask)
    ___ Creativity skills: e.g., arts, writing, acting, thinking, idea generation (specify):

_____
_____

    ___ Other (specify):

_____
_____

4.   What types of jobs or careers do you think would better suit your skills/talents?

_____
_____
_____

5.   What types of jobs or careers do you think would better meet your career/job goals?

_____
_____
_____

Note

In the quiz in Figure 3, there is no reason to limit your selections to 3 jobs in each category. You should list as many as you can think of, but you should only list those you think best meet your stated career and job goals— those that you think would truly inspire you.

You should use the results of the quiz in Figure 3 to begin to think about planning or re-planning your career. You should consciously develop a concrete career or job plan. As with most plans, it needs to be realistic, as well as flexible. In other words, you should aim high, trying to accomplish your career and life goals; but your career plan should also reflect your capabilities and interests.

Figure 4: Your Career or Job Plan

1. List the top two or three career/jobs that you would like to pursue (which could include a new/better position with your current employer).

    _____

    _____

    _____

2. For each of the possible jobs you desire, you need to assess the following:
    *   **Job opportunities** available (check local job listings in the newspaper or online, or with professional or industry newsletters or websites). This will vary by career/job, so you might have to do some investigation. If you're at a loss on where to start, go to your local library and ask the reference librarian for help finding sources. This is not only their job, but most of them are more than willing to help.
    *   Determine average **starting wages/salaries** for the level you would likely start at in these new jobs (entry level, or higher). However, be sure to be reasonable in your estimation, particularly if money is one of your primary motivations to seek a new position.
    *   Investigate **job requirements** for the kind of job you want to pursue. This not only will let you know what qualifications you can emphasize in a job application, but also help you determine what additional training, education or experience you may need to qualify for the job you want. Not meeting minimum qualifications is the easiest, thus usually the first,

factor used by an employer's human resource staff to trim the list of applicants.

3. Determine what it will take for you to meet the qualifications for the job(s) you want.
    - More education/training:
        o What type (college degree; some college; certification; apprenticeship; etc.)?
        o What area to focus on (business, computer, accounting, specific technical knowledge, etc.)?
        o How long will the needed education/training take?
        o Is it possible to achieve these qualifications while still working at your current job?

4. What restrictions or limitations are there to successfully completing your plan?
    - **Geographical location**: Do you need or want to stay in your current location due to personal commitments/relationships (e.g., a significant other's career, parents/family that might need your help, etc.)?
    - **Are there financial costs** to relocate or get the education/training needed?
        o Do you have the funds needed? If so are you willing to invest your money in this new career?
        o If not, are you **willing to borrow money** to improve your career? Remember, education and training for a career should be viewed as an investment, not an expense. You may want to check out possible sources for such a loan before going further in the planning process.
    - Do you **have the time** to pursue the necessary education/training for the new job or career you desire without quitting your current job? If so:
        o How might it hurt your job performance?
        o How much time will it take to complete the training while staying on your current job, and are you willing to invest that amount of time to get the necessary training?
    - Do you have the **financial ability to quit your job** to focus on the necessary training full time so you can start your new career or job sooner rather than later?

5. Based on your answers to #1-4 above, are you still going to consider trying to pursue a new career? Is it a Go___, or No Go___? If it's a "no go," develop a plan to progress in your current job to meet your goals as well as you can, possibly looking at the pursuit of your ideal job as simply delayed until you are in a better position to move ahead with that plan. In the meantime, look for ways to move up in your current job. Talk to your boss or others who are currently in positions above yours about what opportunities might become available and what you would have to do to qualify for such a position. If additional education or training

is needed, see if it is significantly less than what might be required for your "ideal" job, and then make an informed decision on which to pursue.

If it's a "go" to pursue your more ideal job, then you need to develop a specific plan of action: what specific training program to get into, a timetable for both starting and completing such training and for your desired progression in your career—from securing an entry job to the highest position you want to achieve. Obviously the latter will have to be modified periodically based on the actual progress you make and possible changes you make in your life or career goals. You also may need to re-work your time plan from the previous section to account for your new, busier schedule.

Hints for Your Career or Job Plan

- Remember that you are likely to spend at least a third, if not more, of your life working, so it is important not just to do well financially, but also to like the work you do. The best job in the world is the one where you want to go to work, like the people you work with, and often don't even consider what you do as "work." It's worth pursuing a career to attain this if your current job doesn't fit the bill.
- As with most plans, they are not—and should not—be written in stone. Life situations change, sometimes unexpectedly, so life and career goals may also change. You need to periodically review your plan and make updates as necessary, which means your plan should be written down somewhere.
- If you have a significant other, include them in this career planning process. Your career plans are likely to impact, as well as be impacted by, your partner's own plans, especially if they are on a desired career path. As already noted, a change in career not only affects your future financial position but also may significantly impact your current finances, and this needs to be discussed with your partner.
- As with most plans presented in this book, nothing is going to happen unless you develop a plan, and then implement it. So, just do it!
- Consider moving to a new location, even a foreign location, to find the job or career you want to pursue. In 2012, over 6.3 million Americans were working or

studying abroad; the most ever recorded. [19]

- If your career plan involves starting your own business, you need to get as much post-secondary education and job experience as possible that is related to the general area(s) of your business interest before actually pursuing your entrepreneurial venture.

The "Personal Finance" Connection

The finance connection with career and job development should be obvious. You are more likely to work hard and perform at a higher level at a job you like and for which you have some existing talent or skill, which frequently leads to maximizing your earnings (within the earnings range associated with your desired field of work). The time and money spent to further develop your career should be considered an investment, not just an expense. For example, $20,000 spent on career development could easily reap significant future rewards financially as well as in terms of personal satisfaction. In contrast, the same amount of money spent on a new car is an expense that will begin to depreciate in value from the moment you drive the car off the dealer's lot. Furthermore, the more skills or expertise you have, the less expendable you become to your employer; i.e., less likely to be laid off or lose your job and income. Although money may not be your primary concern regarding career, making a good living at something you really like doing will help with most other parts of your life plan.

If you are one of the estimated 50% of Generation Y who wants to start your own business, remember that you will need to save as much money as possible to have some capital to commit to your planned venture (and to help in securing loans or attracting venture capital from potential investors). You also will need to minimize living expenses in order to save that maximum amount of money, not just for your investment, but also to help pay for expenses if you succeed and, at some point, have to either quit your day job or rethink your commitment to your business venture.

Managing and Organizing Your Physical Environment

The Benefits of Organization

Managing your personal physical environment can help create more synergy in your life. It not only helps to reduce stress, but also can assist in managing your time more effectively and ultimately can be a useful tool in managing your money. One of the subtle causes of stress is having a messy physical environment where you can't easily find things in a hurry (keys come to mind), which may result in yelling and screaming, accusations of blame, and having to spend an unacceptable amount of time hunting for needed items. Stress reduction can result not only from having your things and surroundings well organized, but the process of organizing the physical environment also can be satisfying, even motivational; feeling like you are accomplishing something tangible and, more importantly, observable.

We also save time with a well-organized physical environment. It takes less time to find things in an organized office or home. You know where you left your keys, wallet, glasses, checkbook and important papers, or you know where to quickly find a tool you need. Good time management usually leads to a reduction of stress in our personal lives. We get to our destinations on time, and we do not miss important events at work and home.

Managing your physical environment also can lead to monetary savings. Simply knowing what you have (either a mental, written, or video inventory) can save money. We may replace things we think are lost or can't easily find. An organized physical environment also can help us better utilize our possessions. For example, having exercise equipment in an easily accessible area is more likely to lead to frequent use and may keep us from purchasing unneeded replacement items. We even may have hidden treasures that get lost in a messy physical environment: art work, jewelry, collectibles, or just items of significant sentimental value to pass along to the next generation. Some of these items, particularly collectibles, may lose some of their potential value if not kept in a planned, protected place.

Why It's a Problem

This is another one of those skills that busy parents often fail to teach their children. Parents often clean and organize their child's space because it is just easier and faster to do it themselves, thus enabling their children to be poor organizers by not setting and enforcing standards for clean, organized rooms. Or they may do it because they don't think the child can perform this duty "up to their standards." However, it would have been better had parents taught their children to do it, possibly by doing it with them, and enforcing a standard of organization (having rules to follow in this regard), or sanctions for when the rules aren't followed.

Thus, most of us are on our own to learn this important skill to make our lives less stressful. Also, organizing your physical environment not only should help to reduce your stress level and save money, but also help you better manage your time (transferring some of the same organization skills to these different facets of our life). For example, procrastination, a failure to organize the timing of your necessary tasks, whether school, work- or home-related, is not totally dissimilar from misplacing important items.

The Process

If you haven't learned or practiced the skill of organizing, it can be a daunting task. If, on the other hand, you are experienced at organizing some parts of your life, such as your work activities or your time schedule, then you can use the same principles for organizing your physical environment; namely, to follow a logical sequence of activities to accomplish your objective. For example:

- Determine what possessions are most important to you (e.g., family photos, books, heirlooms, antiques, financial papers, sports memorabilia, etc.).
- Locate those important possessions.
- Identify a safe or easily accessible place for these special possessions. If such a space is already in use, hold off moving your special things until later in the process.
- Develop an inventory plan for all other possessions (see **www.knowyourstuff.org** for free home inventory software).

○ List all the storage spaces to go through: closets, drawers, cupboards, attic, loft, shed, garage, basement, etc.

○ Determine how long you want to take to complete the reorganization process. Give yourself enough time that this process does not become an obsession, but don't let it go on and on without a clear end date.

○ Determine what category of goods you want in each available storage space (regardless of what occupies that space now) at the end of this reorganization process.

○ Start the process by going through one storage space at a time. If possible, find a place to store goods that will need to be relocated later when the inventory process is complete (i.e., put things in the basement or garage until you determine where to relocate those goods), but don't put them so far out of sight that you can too easily forget to complete the intended organization project.

○ Get rid of unnecessary items! This may be one of the toughest parts of the process—determining what items you really don't need. With luck, you and your most significant other have opposite tendencies with regard to throwing or saving things. If you live alone, or both have the same tendencies, then be careful to not go to either extreme—saving everything regardless of usefulness, or throwing out things you may want or need later. Throwers need to be very careful not to use their own predilections when dealing with a partner's belongings.

○ Relocate belongings in their designated spaces. If there isn't enough room in the designated space, reconsider the part of the plan where you identify uses for the spaces available. If there still isn't enough room, consider further purging of unnecessary items, renting an off-site storage space, or sending anything stored for others (adult children, friends, other family members) to those people.

○ Periodically go through each storage space to make sure of the integrity of that designation for stored goods. If you find items that don't belong in that space either rectify the problem or modify your plan. However, be warned: simply modifying your plan to accept the appearance of undesignated goods in a space may return you to the myriad of problems caused by an unorganized physical environment.

Organizing Hints

- If in doubt, save. You can always throw things away later, but you cannot easily retrieve things you may have mistakenly discarded. Though I have already confessed to not being a relationship expert, I have first-hand knowledge that this can lead to significant relationship distress.

- Keep one junk drawer, cupboard, or closet. No matter how hard you work at it, there will be some things that just don't fit into a neat category. That's ok. The idea is to have one or two such places, and not to allow all storage places to become unorganized and cluttered with a variety of unrelated items.

- At the end of your reorganization process, consider having a garage sale. Why not get some salvage value out of the things you don't want or need that may have value to others? Whatever is left can be donated to a charity such as Goodwill (who will usually be glad to come and pick up the remaining items as long as they are not simply rubbish). You may be able to take a tax deduction for that contribution, too, if you itemize your tax deductions when filing your tax return.

- For remaining goods that have little if any value, you may need to use whatever means is available to rid yourself of them. If your local area has a "big item" garbage pickup several times a year, then plan your reorganization process to be completed by one of those dates. If not, check and see if there is a private rubbish collector who can remove unwanted goods that have no resale value. And, since it never hurts to help protect our planet, check with your local recycling center to see what you can drop off there.

- Use organizing devices for storage spaces where possible. For example:

- o Closet organizers that allow maximum use of closet space. You can hire people who specialize in closet organization to do this, but you can do it yourself by buying or building similar organizing equipment.
- o Use dividers in cupboards.
- o Put up shelving in basements, attics, lofts, and garages. If you update your kitchen, use the old cupboards in the basement or garage or look for them in garage sales, or even curbside from other peoples' home remodeling projects where old cupboards are being discarded.
- o Consider using plastic bins of various sizes for cupboards, the top shelf in closets, shelves in the garage or basement, or even under the beds.
- Be logical in your planning. Put your keys (house, car office, etc.) in one place. For example, put them nearest the place you most likely would look first, or near the door on a key rack or in a bowl on the counter where everyone knows to put their keys and, more importantly, find them when needed. Another example would be to put all tools either in one place or near where they would normally be used. Both situations save time and help reduce stress.

The "Personal Finance" Connection

Most of you will be absolutely amazed by how good it feels to have your physical environment organized. Though personal satisfaction achieved from being organized may be the biggest reward, it also may help you save money; for example, by not having to replace something you can't find. Avoiding being late for work frequently because you couldn't find a briefcase, important papers, your keys, etc. could even save your job and earning power, thus having a significant impact on your financial position.

Developing a Plan for Health, Fitness, and Appearance

The Benefits of a "Me" Plan

You may be wondering what the heck topics such as health, fitness, and appearance have to do with financial planning. It is important to remember that all the money in the world will not do you or your family much good if you are not in good health. It addition, people who are physically and mentally fit and comfortable with the way they look and feel are more likely to do well in their chosen field of work, thus benefiting financially. If nothing else, they simply have more confidence, energy and motivation to go the extra mile to get things done, to work smarter as well as harder and longer to achieve personal success, however defined.

Consumer Alert!

If you consider getting professional help to reach some of your goals in this section, you may want to weigh the value of self-help versus the cost of professional guidance. For example, those people who have weight loss objectives should remember that diet books, diet centers and related products comprise a multibillion dollar industry that caters to the same people year after year; succeeding financially by their patrons' failures.

If you consider the do-it-yourself method, use common sense and recognize the fact that there is no quick-fix substitute for hard work and reasonable expectations. Do-it-yourself methods can be combined with relatively inexpensive self-help books or advice found in popular magazines or on the Internet. But remember: most people find that free advice is worth every penny they paid for it!

Why It's a Problem

It makes sense that people who do not plan the management of their own health, probably the most important part of their life, are not likely to be motivated or capable of planning their physical environment, career, time usage, or their stress level. While health is most important, fitness and appearance also can impact all other aspects of your life. This category of life planning might best be called your "me" plan, which relates closely to your self-image and level of confidence in dealing with others, affecting, among other things, your ability to succeed in many careers as well as interpersonal relationships.

The Process

First of all, please remember to consult authoritative sources on this subject before developing a specific plan of action for improved health, physical fitness, and especially any permanent alteration of your physical appearance. Also remember that these actions can lead to significant financial expenditures and, thus, relate to money management.

Health, fitness and appearance are not only cosmetic issues, but also may relate directly to the quality or length of your life. They also have a monetary impact in terms of minimizing healthcare costs, including time lost at work due to illness, and even obtaining and maintaining employment in some positions. Thus, the following hints may be useful.

Hints for Health, Fitness, and Appearance

Health
- Most important and simple: even for those in their 20s and 30s, have regular health, dental and eye checkups. We live in a time of increasingly miraculous cures for serious medical issues, but curing almost all of those medical problems requires early diagnosis. If you have dental and vision insurance through your employer, use it. If you don't, buy it (it's not terribly expensive at your age).
- If your employer does not provide disability insurance, buy it yourself. Young people are in accidents, often more than older people because of lifestyle, and sadly, the young are not immune to illnesses that could make it impossible to work.
- Consult a physician to get a check-up to make sure you are able to begin a diet or exercise program and to determine any limitations (and possibly to get suggestions on methods to accomplish your objectives). This is a critical first step for initiating this kind of activity.
- Put health issues above fitness (which are related, of course) and, even more importantly, put both health and

fitness above physical appearance. Even if you are an actor, model, TV personality, etc., looks won't last forever but will remain longer if you are fit and healthy. Many of us seem to prioritize in exactly the opposite direction, even sacrificing health for superficial fitness results such as bulking up muscles with FDA-untested substances or improving our physical appearance through dangerous diets and questionable medical procedures. This is a place where priorities are really important!

Fitness
- Develop, in consultation with a doctor, physical fitness trainer, etc., specific, realistic objectives for improving your physique, weight loss, endurance, etc.
- Determine an appropriate timetable to accomplish your health and fitness objectives (in many instances, in stages of accomplishment at increasingly higher levels).
- Decide on the method(s) you are going to use to accomplish your objectives. This is the time to determine if you are likely to succeed on your own or if you need help. However, carefully review the costs involved. How many people have unused gym memberships or expensive home fitness equipment that is now stored in the attic or basement? Even when used, some products (such as diet supplements) may have questionable effectiveness and may be untested for safety if they do not fall under a specific government regulatory agency.
- If your plan involves the aid of professionals, check them out. Ask for names of current clients, check with your local Better Business Bureau or appropriate licensing board to make sure the person is properly credentialed, and check on their history of complaints filed by previous clients.
- Don't be gullible! You are not going to lose extraordinary amounts of weigh in two or three weeks, nor go from a pear-shaped couch potato to a buffed hunk after six weeks of using an in-home gym (or any device yet known to humankind). Even worse, you are not going to lose weight and get in shape by placing an electronic device around your waist while you sit on the sofa and eat pizza!

- If you are overweight, don't waste your time and money on diets, including diet centers or a book. The most effective diet for otherwise healthy people is easy. Well, easy to tell, not necessarily easy to do. Here's the worst kept secret in the diet world: The best, and probably only way to lose weight and keep it off is to: 1. EAT LESS at each meal. Eat five or six small meals per day rather than two or three big ones; 2. EAT BETTER by watching the saturated fat and calories consumed; and 3. get more PHYSICAL EXERCISE—at least 20-30 minutes of sustained exercise 3-4 times a week, even if that is simply taking a long walk. In addition, eliminate snacking between meals, or begin snacking on fresh fruit and vegetables rather than chips and cookies. If you do these things, you will loose weight and keep it off. It's the LIFESTYLE that must be changed, and changed FOREVER. This paragraph alone could save you hundreds, even thousands of dollars in diet books, programs, diet centers, etc., and it's guaranteed to work if you just do it.

- Exercise with your significant other or friends. It is something almost everyone can do, albeit at different levels of intensity and even if they have somewhat different objectives. You can spur each other on to continue to follow your action plan, and thus, will be more likely to do it regularly. Doing this with a significant other has the added benefit of helping maintain a good relationship—having something you can do together. Not only doing the activity, but also talking about it, even jointly planning the on-going activity.

Note to Dieters

If you join a *free* center or support group, that may be a good idea, but if they charge a membership fee and sell you their diet products, you probably will be better off getting together with your own group of friends who also want to lose weight, get in shape, etc. Exercise together at your homes and share healthy food recipes, which is free and probably more fun.

- Don't waste your money! Try a gym that has a "trial" program to see if you will really use it over a month or two, or try out the types of machines that you want to purchase for home use BEFORE you buy them. Also, don't hesitate to ask friends if you can try out their equipment to see what works for you. And, of course, there is always good used equipment in the classifieds section of the newspaper, on Internet sites such as eBay and Craigslist, and at some garage sales, usually at very good prices for near-new items.
- If you find that you are devoting an inordinate amount of time on physical fitness, you need to reconsider your priorities. At least consider a downward revision of your objectives and expectations. You may have been overreaching with this one aspect of your total life.
- You should set a reasonable monthly budget limit on your expenditures for fitness products and services, including gym memberships and personal trainers.

Appearance

Appearance is more than just personal vanity. While this may seem to be somewhat superficial to some people, a better appearance can increase self-esteem and confidence, which can improve your ability to find a job or get a promotion at your current job. It also can help you enjoy life more by being comfortable interacting with coworkers and friends, which can help a career but, more importantly, help reduce stress and related health issues. There are some relatively simple changes that could make a real difference in one's desired appearance at relatively little cost. For example:

- Clothes (appropriate wardrobe for age and occupation)
- Hairstyle (again, appropriate for age and occupation)
- Clean, unstained teeth (but probably not the scary whiteness so many TV personalities have). Today, even more significant dental issues can be corrected with relative ease and safety (for example, nearly invisible braces to correct crooked adult teeth).
- New glasses or contacts. Some people actually look better in glasses, but for those who do not, contact lenses are a relatively easy and a somewhat low-cost change that can

have a real impact (even change the color appearance of your eyes). If you wear glasses, new ones should be both age and occupationally appropriate. Style should be current but, for most jobs, not too trendy.

- Personal hygiene. An awkward but important issue to bring up, good personal hygiene is expected in our society, and poor hygiene WILL detract from your appearance and the image you convey to others and could, among other problems, keep you from getting or keeping a job, as well as social friends. Important hygiene items include:
  o Regular bathing (daily for those without dry skin problems)
  o Clean fingernails
  o Clean teeth (brushed and flossed after each meal if possible; if not, use other over-the-counter methods such as the finger brush as a stop-gap measure)
  o Clean hair (regardless of style, dirty hair is a turnoff to work colleagues and clients)
  o Very limited use of cologne and perfumes. What may smell good to you may be very unpleasant to others. If you do use these products, it should be in very small amounts, just enough to give a hint of odor.
  o Use antiperspirant/deodorant. Odorless is best, and many people need the combination of the two ingredients, especially anyone who is physically active.

The benefits of a better appearance, both personally and professionally, are many. You can gain confidence (a better self-image and probably an improvement in how others see you). It also can help your career. The clothes may not make the man or woman, but it helps if they are clean, reasonably stylish, and age and occupationally appropriate. As noted, good personal hygiene is also an important work-related appearance factor to consider. That, along with the other personal appearance factors, could improve interpersonal relationships or opportunities to develop new ones, expanding your social circles.

Note

Obviously there are other personal health, fitness, and appearance issues that you may have to deal with or want to consider, but the ones presented here are those that this author can present within his areas of experience and expertise, and that have a clear relationship to career and personal finance.

It is also important that you develop reasonable expectations of what is possible in these life-planning categories to avoid over-spending and achieve personal satisfaction.

The "Personal Finance" Connection

Many products and services associated with health, physical fitness, and appearance can be expensive, and thus need to be considered in terms of other needs and definitely as part of financial budget planning, particularly for recurring expenses (e.g., monthly fitness center fees). However, these personal improvements also may relate to career development, which can obviously have a major impact on your ability to meet financial goals.

This category of life planning is particularly susceptible to the financial problem of wasting money on unnecessary items and services that don't work or don't work as well as advertised, or where the objectives could be reached more simply and inexpensively. Do not hesitate to return any product that does not work for you. Most companies that produce or sell consumer products and services make that part of their offer, so take advantage of that feature (but remember to always keep receipts of purchases until you are sure you are fully satisfied). You also need to periodically reassess your need for many of these products and services; e.g., if you are not using your gym membership, you need to quit and try to get a refund or determine how to manage your time better in order to make use of that service.

Disclaimer

Yes, I know, I'm providing self-help lists throughout this book, even after chastising authors of "quick-fix" books for using this simplistic method. The difference is that the lists in this book are offered as examples, guidelines, ideas, or suggestions that can be taken, or not, at the discretion of the reader—not as a specific formula or recipe for success. All an author can do is give readers some ideas that might help them in their life planning process. The important thing is that you are thinking about the process, including your goals, as well as your specific courses of action.

Interpersonal Relationships

The Benefits of Interpersonal Relationships

We humans are social creatures. Most of us need and seek out interpersonal connections. Social interaction with a group of close friends helps to stabilize our lives and can make them richer. Medical studies have shown that people who have more frequent interaction with friends not only live longer, but also enjoy life more. These people tend to have less stress, and when they are stressed, having friends helps alleviate the negative effects of stress. People without close friendships often rate their satisfaction with life much lower than those with friends.

Why It's a Problem

Our modern world has made long-term friendships more difficult. Gen Y-ers will move more often and have a greater number of different jobs in their lifetime than any previous generation. Your generation is not only more likely to wander further from home to a different city or state to find desirable employment opportunities, but also to different countries as more jobs are created in developing countries and as more U.S. jobs are outsourced globally.

The more often you change jobs and locations, the less time you spend with the same group of co-workers and neighbors. The farther you move from your original home, the less personal face-to-face interaction you will have with family and old friends. Previous generations often let their old best friends drift away because of geographical distance or just neglect. We should probably remember that old friends usually make the best friends due to common histories. That is probably why so many people have siblings as good, even best friends, which may be nice; however, the problem with that is the "family baggage" and responsibility they might also bring to the relationship. The upside of family is that they usually will be brutally honest with us, but old friends may have the same honesty without the same baggage.

Gen Y is the first generation that has the social networking technology to stay in close touch with friends, even those who are located far away. So there is no good reason to let those friendships fade. On the other hand, that same technology has some potential pitfalls: 1. your generation is able to stay connected with work and everyone else you know 24/7/365, even when trying to relax or on vacation—i.e. you rarely disconnect; 2. social networking sites tempt people to post both words and pictures that you might regret later, particularly if your current or prospective employers look at those sites, as well as other businesses such as insurance companies; and 3. some of these postings could haunt you for many years (think of attempting to run for political office at some point in life with a traceable history of social network postings).

Some people will turn down job opportunities or promotions that involve moving, even ones that may significantly improve their financial position, in order to stay close to family and friends. Others will take those employment opportunities for a number of reasons including, for example, an improvement in earning potential, but may suffer more stress and anxiety during personal and professional difficulties without the safety net a close support group can provide. Ultimately, this is something that you may have to determine for yourself. However, as a very mobile generation, you also are more likely to make a concerted effort to establish new friendships wherever you end up.

The Process

We need to be aware of the importance of maintaining good interpersonal relationships at work, socially, and at home. Each of us should assess how well we are doing in this regard and, if necessary, get help resolving interpersonal problems we identify. Developing and maintaining good interpersonal relationships can dramatically impact your quality of life.

At Work

- **Co-workers**. This is a group of people with whom you really need to get along. In fact that should have been a major factor in whether or not you accepted the offer for employment. Not only is it more fun to go to work with people you actually enjoy being around, but it also tends to improve your performance. The trend in most organizations is towards more teamwork. You will have to collaborate with co-workers on projects to which you are assigned, and your group results largely will be determined by how well your collaboration worked. Coworkers also can be helpful as:
  o an informal source of communication regarding issues at work;
  o people with whom you can brainstorm work-related ideas;
  o a pool of people with whom you may want to socialize (especially important if your job is not close to where you grew up or went to school);
  o a group that may be involved in determining whether you get a promotion. They may well be asked how well you got along with them, whether or not you were cooperative on work projects, etc.
- **Your superiors**. This is a different issue. A good cordial relationship is very useful, but a personal relationship with a boss can be awkward at times. However, if handled well, with clear boundaries defined, it also could benefit your career.
- **Your subordinates**. This can be a critical factor in promotions. People who get along with and support the efforts of their subordinates are seen as leaders, people who empower and listen to subordinates, create reasonable expectations of performance, and work to help them succeed.

Most recommendation forms that your references for a new position or job will be asked to fill out include questions about how well you get along with others. While positive answers to this question may not be sufficient to clinch a new position, negative answers can keep you from further consideration.

Non-Work Friends

It may be useful to have a group of friends who you don't work with so that work is not always on your mind, and so your significant other doesn't feel as though they are being left out of conversations. These friends provide you with a nice social outlet that falls somewhere between co-workers and family, where work problems aren't discussed and family issues aren't in the way of having a good, relaxing time. The longer you have the same group of friends, the more they become a stable support group that can improve the quality of your life, possibly for the rest of your life.

We all need friends, possibly couples, as adult playmates and confidants who are not connected to work. It's probably best if they are not our next-door neighbors because that proximity creates a whole set of other issues that often preclude "best friend" status (but if it works for you, go for it). We really need friends who we can hang out with and do the non-family, non-work things that we are interested in (golf, tennis, sports activities, spectator sports, shopping, sightseeing, etc.). As already noted, medical research even suggests that having and maintaining good friends keeps us alive longer. I am equally sure their counsel and support helps reduce stress, again improving both physical and mental health.

As noted earlier, there is no need to let old friends fade away. The positive opportunity for your generation to stay in touch with old friends, maintaining those relationships over a lifetime, offers an opportunity to achieve all the benefits of such relationships noted above. But, once again, you should use discretion in what kinds of messages and pictures you send through social media.

Family

This, of course, could be your most important group of confidants, with whom you probably have the most history and sometimes the closest relationships. It also is the group where problems that arise are most difficult and may have the most profound effect upon you; your mood, attitude, feelings of self-worth, and generally how good you feel about your life. It also can affect your finances if family members need help from you, or if you need help from family. Personal loans to family members can cause relationship problems that add a great deal of stress to your life whether you are the lender or borrower.

When family problems arise, they must be taken care of as soon as possible. Don't allow these problems to fester. Good interpersonal communication often can help resolve problems, but if not, you and your significant other (or whatever family member is involved) should get professional help to try to resolve any issue that could affect your relationship. Estrangement between family members is not only sad, but also can impact your mental and physical well-being. Do not take these relationships for granted, but do not let them get away from you for lack of contact, or because of unresolved issues. For most of you, family relationships will be the most important ones for the long term.

As with old friends, social networking can be an easy and inexpensive way to stay in touch with parents, siblings, cousins, etc., even if you live far away from these folks. But remember, if you "friend" a family member, they may end up having access to other postings you have on social media, so as a good rule of thumb, never post anything that you wouldn't want your Mom or Dad to see!

Hints for Interpersonal Relationships

- Making friends may come naturally for many of you, but for those to whom it doesn't come naturally or easily, you need to make a concerted effort.
  - o Join a sports team or some other group activity that interests you in order to meet people.
  - o Volunteer for some charity or cause that you are passionate about.
  - o Join some professional organization in your community that is not comprised of co-workers.

Note

All of the above suggestions have a common benefit: they all will lead to a group activity where you will have at least one big thing in common with everyone else in the group.

- Socialize with co-workers at appropriate times away from work. They usually will invite some non-coworkers with whom you might connect.
  - o Try not to let family and co-workers (even ones you like and consider to be friends) become your total social network. Many adult males (and increasingly working females) do not maintain strong personal friendships outside of their family or workplace, and those can be important "independent" relationships.
- Don't become a weekend agoraphobic—not going too far from home unless it involves Home Depot, the grocery store, or kid's activities, often neglecting "adult play time." Remember, you will benefit from adult contact and conversation that has nothing to do with work or family issues. It's a stress reducer and simply is likely to offer more social stimulation in your life, getting you out of the house and doing more than you might do otherwise.

The "Personal Finance" Connection

The finance connection with interpersonal relationships is not quite as clear as it was for some other life planning topics; however, there is a connection. If you don't relate well with other people it may affect your job—even researchers have to work and collaborate with other researchers, bosses, and probably some subordinates. A good co-worker relationship can improve your chances of promotions and related increases in income. It also can lead to new job opportunities. Good relationships with family and non-work friends can be good for our health, reducing stress and minimizing both medical and psychological difficulties, which may reduce health-related costs that you incur. People with good friends tend to be happier and have a more positive outlook on life, which, in turn, helps maintain a good attitude and level of enthusiasm at work.

As a general rule, don't lend or borrow money from friends or relatives. Financial dealings can permanently harm personal relationships. That said, if you choose to lend money to friends or relatives, only lend an amount you are willing and can afford to lose if you were not paid back or not paid as soon as originally promised. If you borrow money from a friend or relative, pay it back as soon as possible, as your number one priority other than paying current expenses and replenishing your emergency savings. It probably would be best for your personal relationship if both parties sign a written agreement (promissory note) with a witness, specifying the amount of the loan, the interest rate to be paid (if any) and the repayment schedule with a specific beginning and ending time period. Such a document could help prevent future disputes over the terms of the loan and make it clear to both parties that this is a legal as well as personal agreement. (Go to **www.lawdepot.com** for an appropriate legal form.)

7. Managing Your Personal Finances
Finally, let's talk about your money!

Note

Many Americans, particularly younger financially inexperienced people, are not financially literate. That is, they are not familiar with financial terms used. Thus, a glossary of selected terms used in this section can be found in Appendix 1.

In the previous discussions about various aspects of a life plan, the financial implications were presented. In each case, the potential financial benefits of doing a good job in planning other parts of your life were apparent, but the opposite should be equally clear. If you don't plan the non-financial components of your life well, it not only could offset the benefits you might gain from doing a good job of financial planning, but it also could make that planning even more difficult to do than it would be otherwise.

Handling all the financial issues in your life is no easy task. You need to have a clear understanding of your financial goals, as well as near-term objectives. These are critical to both developing a clear plan, as well as assessing your current position in order to have a clear idea of where you are now (the starting point for the plan). You also should have a good understanding of your current expenses and income, hopefully based on keeping good records, as well as a clear idea of your assets and liabilities (debts); when taken together, showing your current net worth. For many young people, net worth will actually be a negative figure: having more debt than the cumulative worth of your assets, at least for a few years into your first career or job.

Implementing the plan to achieve your financial goals may take a great deal of time and effort. Remember, a good plan that is poorly implemented is still likely to fail, and this is not a one-time effort. Financial planning needs to be an on-going process that becomes a regular part of your life, not just until retirement, but until you can no longer do it for yourself or there is no longer any need to do so.

The good news is that a carefully thought out financial plan, executed well, can make your life much happier and may make other aspects of your life much easier. Taking money problems out of the picture for other life decisions you need to make can reduce the intensity of those decisions and allow you to focus on other important considerations. For example, looking at new job opportunities without worrying about whether the new employer will pay the bulk of your moving costs, which might otherwise have affected your decision to accept a job offer.

Developing a Financial Plan

Your finances not only need to be planned carefully, but also should be written so that you can review them when needed. Financial planning, as you are about to see, involves much more than budgeting your current income. It also includes an assessment of your current financial position relative to the financial goals you should already have established, as well as managing your debt, reducing your expenses, and saving/investing for future wants and needs.

Revisit your financial goals and objectives.

At this point you should reaffirm your financial goals and objectives. If you established those goals for the first time after starting to read this book, you should go back and review them after you have looked carefully at your non-financial life plans. If they remain the same, that's fine. This is called active non-change, which means you decided not to change your goals after an active review to determine if they need to be changed due to other circumstances in your life or recognition that they originally may have been set too high or too low. This review must be both of your long-term financial goals and short-term financial objectives.

Review your current overall financial position.

Once you have determined your net worth by completing the worksheet below, you will have a clearer picture of your current financial position and be able to compare your financial position with your financial goals. Thus, you can better assess what you need to do with your current monthly budget to start to better meet those goals.

Net Worth Worksheet

ASSETS

1. Short term (liquid/cash) assets:
   - \$_____ checking account balance(s):
   - \$_____ savings (money market) account balances
   - \$_____ Certificate of Deposit balances
   - \$_____ money hidden in a jar or under the mattress (which should immediately be put into one of the above)

   - \$_____ Total

2. Long-term financial investment assets (current market value):
   - \$_____ individually-owned stock, bonds and mutual funds (in a brokerage account or held by you), but not those that are part of a designated retirement account
   - \$_____ in an IRA (Individual Retirement Account)
   - \$_____ 401-k (or 403-b) tax-deferred mutual fund retirement accounts (403-b are similar to 401-k plans, but used in certain occupations such as teachers' and college professors' state-sponsored retirement programs)
   - \$_____ other investments (specify):
     - \$_____ -- _____
     - \$_____ -- _____

3. Real-estate (current market value):
   - \$_____ house
   - \$_____ 2nd house (summer home, time share, etc.)
   - \$_____ unimproved land
   - \$_____ rental property
   - \$_____ other (specify):
     - \$_____ -- _____
     - \$_____ -- _____

4. Precious metals (other than stock holdings in precious metals) at current market value:
   - \$_____ gold
   - \$_____ silver

$_____other (specify):
$_____ -- _____
$_____ -- _____

5. Other personal property (salable items of significant value):
$_____ antiques of real value (appraised value)
$_____ art (appraised value)
$_____ jewelry (appraised value)
$_____ other collectibles (specify):
$_____ -- _____
$_____ -- _____

6. Automobiles, boats, etc. (current market value):
$_____ autos
$_____ boats
$_____ RVs
$_____ other (specify):
$_____ -- _____
$_____ -- _____

7. Other (specify):
$_____ -- _____
$_____ -- _____

Total Assets: $_____

LIABILITIES

$_____ college loans (current balance)
$_____ credit card balances (bankcards, store cards, gas cards, etc.)
$_____ auto loan/lease balance
$_____ other installment loans (furniture, electronics, etc.)
$_____ personal loan balances (from family or friends)
$_____ home mortgage
$_____ home equity loans
$_____ other (specify):
$_____ -- _____
$_____ -- _____

Total Liabilities: $_____

NET WORTH

$_____ Total Assets
- $_____ Total Liabilities
_____
= $_____ **NET WORTH**

You should keep a file (preferably a computer file, with a backup file elsewhere) listing all of the above accounts and loans by name and numbers, as well as information on the location of ownership documents (titles of ownership), etc. to facilitate your own periodic review, as well as important information in case of your illness or death. Also, for valuables that need to be appraised, this should be done not just for your assessment of value for your financial plan, but also because these items need to be insured and you will need an appraisal in order to obtain the proper insured value.

When assessing your current, overall financial position, don't be too surprised if you find that you have a negative net worth. As noted earlier, many young people, especially those with loans for post-high school education or training, are likely to have significant debt early in their career and, conversely, not many short- or long-term assets. Your financial planning for the future should help you not only achieve a positive net worth, but also move towards meeting all your financial goals.

Assess your monthly expenses relative to income.

Once you know your financial position, you need to use the income / expense worksheet below (or one similar to it) to assess your current monthly income, the expenses you incur each month, and the resulting savings you are able to achieve. This is a necessary step in order to establish a budget that is reasonable (workable) and that can help you achieve, or better achieve, both short-term objectives and long-term financial goals.

Income / Expense Worksheet

AFTER-TAX MONTHLY INCOME

$_____ Your income (after taxes and all other deductions from paycheck)
$_____ Significant other's income (after tax and all deductions)
$_____ All other "regular" sources of income (spousal support, child support, rent, monthly dividends/interest, etc.) after deductions, including taxes.

_____

$_____ **TOTAL AFTER-TAX MONTHLY INCOME**

REGULAR MONTHLY EXPENSES

$_____ Mortgage/rent payment
$_____ House maintenance/repair
$_____ Total utilities:
     $_____ gas
     $_____ electricity
     $_____ phone
     $_____ cable
     $_____ internet
     $_____ other (specify _____)
$_____ Total transportation:
     $_____ car payment/lease (if any)
     $_____ car expenses (repairs, general maintenance/service)
     $_____ gas
     $_____ parking (work and home) or
     $_____ public transportation cost for work/etc.
$_____ Total insurance:
     $_____ life
     $_____ health (including prescription/dental/vision)
     $_____ disability
     $_____ homeowners/condo/renters
     $_____ auto
     $_____ other (specify _____)
$_____ Uninsured medical expenses (co-pays/deductibles/etc.)
$_____ Groceries and household cleaning items
$_____ Total personal spending:
     $_____ entertainment
     $_____ travel
     $_____ clothes
     $_____ gifts
     $_____ personal care items
$_____ Miscellaneous expenses
$_____ Pay-off of credit cards/loans
$_____ Other (specify)

$_____ **TOTAL MONTHLY EXPENSES**

MONTHLY SAVINGS

  $_____ **Total Monthly Income**
- $_____ **Total Monthly Expenses**
_____

= $_____ **Monthly Savings**

Total Monthly Savings

To get a clear picture of how much you actually are saving per month (to see how well you are achieving your financial objectives for the year, as well as long-term goals), you should add up: 1. how much money you have left after all expenses are paid per month that you are able to place in a savings account (or in longer-term after-tax investments such as government bonds, certificates of deposit, stocks, corporate bonds, etc.); and 2. any pre-tax funds you had withheld from your paycheck per month that are placed in a retirement investment account: 401 (k), 403(b), Keogh Plan , etc.

$_____   After-tax money placed in savings (or after-tax investments) from the Income / Expense worksheet.

$_____   Pre-tax investment money automatically deducted from income (e.g., 401k/403b/Keogh Plan retirement plans)

$_____   **TOTAL SAVINGS/MONTH**

If you are keeping your monthly after-tax savings (money earned/month above total expenses) in a checking account or, worse, in cash, you should consider placing it in a savings account or money market account to earn some interest on those savings or some other longer-term investments if the funds are not needed as a safety net for emergencies or other unanticipated expenses (a later section in the book will discuss these investment options in more detail).

Although the "total" savings/month figure above is probably most accurate in terms of assessing your overall financial position (helping assess how well you are meeting financial goals) it is best, for budget planning purposes, to focus on the savings amount remaining/month from income after all expenses are paid.

Develop a monthly budget.

You should use the above information to develop a budget—or for some of you, to review and possibly revise your old budget. The information you recorded should be, among other things, enlightening in terms of how you are spending your money. If you found it difficult to figure out how much you spend per category, then you are not keeping good enough records of your expenditures. Similarly, you should be keeping a copy of your income statements. If not, start doing so immediately so you know your gross income, all deductions your employer makes and, finally, your "take home pay" after all taxes and other deductions.

If you are one of the many who probably did have some difficulty figuring out how much you spend, then start now to keep a record of all expenditures for at least one or two months in order to continue with the financial planning process. However, in the meantime it might be a good idea to estimate what you think you spend in each category. Then, after recording your expenses and income for a month or two, re-do the above assessment and compare it with what you thought you spent. Once you have done this, you will be particularly well prepared (and hopefully motivated) to continue the financial planning process, especially if what you thought you spent per month was much less than what you actually spent, both overall and per expense category.

After recording your current income and expenses, you need to assess your ability to save or invest monthly relative to your short-term financial objectives (which must be met in order to meet your long-term financial goals). Then you need to ask yourself if you are moving in the right direction and at a pace that is likely to achieve your long-term financial goals by some stipulated age or point in your life. If not, then you need to see how you can increase income (see section below) or reduce your expenses and save more in the short run. In both cases, the best short-run financial tool to use is a monthly budget, with a similar structure to the previous section where you reviewed your current income and expenses.

How To Construct an Actual Budget

If you already have a written budget, then you need to review it and determine if it is working for you (the above assessment of expenses relative to income should help in that determination). If it is working well and you are meeting short-term objectives and are on track to achieve long-term financial goals, good for you. Keep following it! If not, you need to revise your existing budget using the ideas presented below.

Whether you are revising an existing budget or developing a monthly budget for the first time, start with the same format that was used above to record your current expenses. Make sure your budget is at least as detailed as the categories used in the above assessment of monthly income and expenses. Consider adding categories not listed that you added under "other." The more detailed, the better you will be able to assign the appropriate amount of your monthly income to the expenses you are incurring, and to find places where you might be able to reduce expenses and either reallocate money to other categories that are underfunded or, even better, add more to savings and investments. (See Appendix 4: Sample Budget Plan)

Don't be too dismayed when you realize that many expense categories reflect "fixed" expenses, at least in the short-run. Focus on how much you spend in the more discretionary expense line items such as entertainment, personal spending, etc. as well as in the "necessary, but not fixed" expense categories such as groceries, car expenses, etc., which usually are conducive to reasonable expenditure reductions even in the short run (see the section on spending hints below).

As you revise or develop your new monthly financial budget, remember the general characteristics of effective budgets discussed earlier:

- **Flexibility**. If you try to budget to the last penny with no leeway for unexpected expenses or changes in income, then your budget is doomed to fail. Unanticipated events occur and unfortunate things happen in everyone's life, and they often have financial consequences. Ask your parents or older siblings what is often their most difficult expense to handle, not to mention to budget for, and the answer is almost always the "unexpected." While the monthly budget may not be able to handle all such events that might occur, it will help in two ways: 1. if flexibility is built into a budget with a line item such as "miscellaneous" with some amount allocated to that item each month (whether or not it was used in past months), most unexpected events can be handled when they arise; and 2. additional flexibility is added by making an effort to save money every month above and beyond a miscellaneous line item or tax-deferred investments automatically withheld from paychecks, so that these unexpected events usually can be financed without increasing debt; or, if not needed for the latter, can help build up your liquid savings for future unexpected events.

- **Realistic**. The allocation of your monthly income needs to be realistic. Most financial planners suggest that you should pay yourself first; in other words, save a certain percentage of each after-tax (and other withholdings) paycheck. You should save as much as possible; a minimum of 5%, preferably 10%, and more ideally 15-20%. A good idea, but if it leads to allocating insufficient amounts of monthly income to things such as groceries and household items, or even entertainment, the budget is likely to fail. However, if saving is simply relegated to what's left at the end of the month, you are not likely to meet your short or long-term financial goals. So try to establish a savings amount per month in your budget that you consider to be reasonable relative to your income (and reevaluate that % periodically, hopefully finding ways to increase it over time). While tax-deferred savings and investments, such as an automatic deduction from your pay check in a 401(k), are best, you also need to fund a savings account for those unexpected expenses and for those wants that we all desire to improve our quality of life.

- **Written**. If the budget you create is so simple you can keep it in your head without putting it in print, then your budget is too simple. If your budget is as specific as suggested in this book, then you would have to have an amazing memory to be able to accurately recall the amount allocated for each item, but most of us do not have that good of a memory. It also is important for you to be able to share your budget with significant others in order that everyone is on the same financial planning page. Thus a written—or computer-generated—budget is absolutely required.

Either use a pencil for initial planning, or make several copies of this worksheet. Even better, develop one on a spreadsheet such as Excel, or purchase one of the many personal finance and budgeting software programs sold commercially (for example: *Microsoft Money* or *Quicken*). But be sure it is one that you find logical, intuitive and generally user-friendly.

Note

It is a good idea to use the month in which your income is normally adjusted by your employer for any salary or wage increase as the beginning of your budget year since a change in income requires a change in your budget; hopefully in savings. If there is no regular schedule for increases in income, then it would make sense to use the normal calendar year since that is at least consistent with the tax year.

Budget Worksheet

AFTER-TAX MONTHLY INCOME (the same info you put in the previous exercise):

$_____ Your "net" income (after taxes and all other deductions from paycheck)

$_____ Significant other's income (after tax and all deductions)

$_____ All other "regular" sources of income (spousal support, child support, rent, monthly dividends/interest, etc.)

= $_____ **TOTAL AFTER-TAX MONTHLY INCOME**

REGULAR MONTHLY EXPENSES

Some of your monthly expenses are not controllable in the short-run, so for now they will be the same as in the previous exercise. However, for those that are not fixed, you need to see where you can reduce expenses. Remember, if your employer pays some of your expenses, ONLY include the amount, if any, that you pay "out of pocket" for those expenditures per month.

$_____ Mortgage/rent payment

$_____ House maintenance/repair

$_____ Total utilities:

    $_____ gas

    $_____ electricity

    $_____ phone

    $_____ cable

    $_____ internet

    $_____ other (specify _____)

$_____ Total transportation:

    $_____ car payment/lease (if any)

    $_____ car expenses (repairs, general maintenance/service)

    $_____ gas

$_____ parking (work and home) or
$_____public transportation cost for work/etc.
$_____ Total insurance:
     $_____ life
     $_____ health (including prescription/dental/vision)
     $_____ disability
     $_____ homeowners/condo/renters
     $_____ auto
     $_____ other (specify_____)
$_____ Uninsured medical expenses (co-pays/deductibles/etc.)
$_____ Groceries and household cleaning items
$_____ Total personal spending:
     $_____ entertainment
     $_____ travel
     $_____ clothes
     $_____ gifts
     $_____ personal care items
$_____ Miscellaneous expenses
$_____ Pay-off of credit cards/loans
$_____ Other (specify)

$_____ **TOTAL MONTHLY EXPENSES**

$_____ **Net Income** *minus* **Expenses = "Planned Savings" / Month**

Reminder

In a perfect budget, savings would be planned first, before expenses are budgeted. However, for bookkeeping purposes, savings logically appears at the end of a budget as the figure remaining after expenses are deducted from income.

Bookkeeping aside, for your budget planning purposes, first determine how much you want to save/month, then try to work the rest of your planned budget accordingly so that you end up with your planned savings amount after all expenditures.

Start using your new or revised budget.

Hopefully, you haven't given up on financial planning due to the work required. I warned you this wouldn't be easy, but the benefits can be remarkable: learning to live within your means, saving money for unanticipated expenses, paying down any debt you have accumulated, saving to meet future goals, not to mention the peace of mind that financial stability provides. Of course, once again, for this to happen you actually have to create and FOLLOW your budget.

Keep track of actual expenditures.

You should keep track of actual expenditures during the month (ultimately to compare your actual expenditures with what you budgeted) and do this every month until you know whether or not the budget is working for you.

If there is a positive discrepancy in an expense item, you are actually spending less than you budgeted, so add that to your "planned savings/month" item in the budget. If you find a negative discrepancy, then you need to either reduce your spending on that expense item where possible (preferable), or change your budget (find areas where you can reduce expenditures, or expenses items where you currently are spending less than budgeted, to make up the difference). Only as a last resort should you reduce your current monthly savings. But, of course, that would be better than going into debt or not paying your monthly bills.

Review the budget periodically, and revise if necessary.

Even if your current monthly budget is working well (actual expenses the same or less than budgeted expenses), you need to review your budget periodically. Sometimes expenses change (unfortunately, more often in the higher rather than lower direction), and your income may change (hopefully in a positive direction, but both positive and negative changes require a modification in your budget). We are, of course, talking about permanent/continuing changes. For example, a one-time negative change in expenses should be handled by taking money from a "miscellaneous" or "savings" account.

However, you also need to revise the income part of your budget if there is a permanent change. Whereas a one-time increase in income (e.g., tax refund) should go immediately into either a savings account or to reduce debt, a permanent change in income should, ideally, also go into beefing up current savings to meet short-term objectives (having a financial safety net) and to paying off debt, particularly credit card debt. Once those objectives are met, then the fun starts; you can add money to the discretionary expenses in your budget or your near-term wants such as: vacations, more entertainment, a new car, etc. Once your finances are stable, you then can budget for those wants, almost as though they are personal escrow accounts within your savings for each "want item," and eventually purchase them without incurring debt.

Improving Your Financial Position

There are only a few basic methods to improve your financial position, though obviously, there may be a number of individual actions you could take within each method. Other than winning the lottery or inheriting a large sum of money (both of which have a very low probability of occurring for most people), you can improve your financial position by: 1. increasing your income; 2. reducing your spending; and 3. reducing or eliminating debt.

Increasing income.

One of the first methods many people consider in order to improve their financial position is to increase income, if possible.

Monthly wages/salaries

This might be increased by: seeking an increase in pay from your current employer (or working to improve job performance to obtain the maximum possible regular annual or bi-annual salary increase); seeking a second job (if it doesn't conflict with your current position); seeking a new job at a higher salary; encouraging a stay-home significant other, if any, to consider getting a job; or pursuing an entrepreneurial passion that has revenue possibilities. Not all of the above options will increase income immediately, but they can over time make a significant improvement in your total income.

Earnings on savings/investments

You might be able to increase your current earnings from interest-bearing checking and savings accounts and other liquid investments. For example, seek out higher interest rates on checking and savings accounts or certificates of deposit. Check bank rates online or talk to your current bank representative. Depending on how much money you keep in those accounts and CDs, you could conceivably add income to your monthly budget, so this might be worth checking out.

However, you should NOT look at earnings from any investment portfolios you might have in order to increase current income in the short run. Such funds, which hopefully are invested in tax-deferred accounts, should be looked at annually to review earnings, but those earnings should be left in those accounts (though possibly reallocated among securities with the advice of a financial planner) in order to grow and compound your long-term investments, which will be discussed in more detail in an upcoming section. In fact, there could be tax and early withdrawal implications for tax-deferred long-term investments (though a few have "borrowing provisions" for some special cases, such as buying a house or paying for education).

Looking for ways to increase income is always a good idea, but not the easiest way to improve your financial position in the short-run. A salary or wage increase may be beyond your control, other than performing your job as well as possible and making sure your superiors are aware of your performance. New jobs, or promotions on your current job, may require relocation, which may be a good idea and may offer a significant increase in short-term earnings, but also may cause major disruptions in other aspects of your life (and your family's life). That said, in the long run, career development can be one of the best ways to significantly improve your financial position, which is why planning your career development is such an important part of managing your life.

Manage expenses and spending.

Some might phrase this section as finding the "sweet spot" between austerity and extravagance. In either case, the best method to accomplish this in the short run is to find ways to minimize your monthly expenses by better managing spending. But, it also is true that managing spending can help improve your long-term financial position. You might be able to find ways to change your lifestyle that can permanently reduce your living expenses.

Minimize expenses in the short-run.

Shop smarter (general hints)

There are a number of steps you can take to shop smarter; specifically, wasting less time and money and getting more bang for your buck.

- Plan multi-task trips (saves money and time) by doing as many chores in one trip as possible given time and distance. For example: you could incorporate the following tasks into one trip: get gas; grocery shop (or pick up a few extra groceries while at a gas station that is also a convenience store); and visit family or friends (offer to pick up some grocery items for them if they can't easily do this for themselves). You get the idea!

- Have a shopping list and stick to the list as much as possible. Try to avoid impulse items unless you see something that should (honestly) have been on the list.

- Look for sales/coupons. While some people might overdo this, a bit of diligence in collecting coupons that easily come to you via mail, newspapers, magazines, etc. can, if used regularly, save a tremendous amount of money on items such as groceries, prescriptions and clothing. Just being observant enough to cut out coupons from Sunday papers and only for brands of items you would normally purchase can on average save a family of four $2000/year or more.

- Try not to be brand conscious and you can save even more money. Decide which stores or online sites to shop at where you have found the general quality and price of their merchandise to fit your budget and tastes. It also may make you more comfortable if you inquire what nationally-known company produced the retailer's private label item. You also should buy generic where possible (e.g., prescription drugs), offered at significantly lower prices.

- Shop for specific items that you need. Shopping just to "look" in stores or online is not a good pastime because it often leads to buying items you didn't plan on buying and probably could do without.

- Shop for best value (best product for the price) and wait

for sales. Don't buy when you don't absolutely need an item unless it's an emergency good. However, this requires anticipation of wants and needs.

- Know the unit price for goods based on weight/volume or some other measurement and then compare prices of similar products.
- Try to find acceptable pre-owned products for durable goods, such as autos, exercise equipment, furniture, etc.
- Be willing not to buy if you don't find exactly what you want.
- Take some time and money to get information on products and services before spending your money.
  - o Spend money to get valuable information to help you make better purchases; again, better value purchase in terms of quality and price relationship. This can help you save money when buying desired products and also minimize buyer's remorse. You can either subscribe to consumer journals with product ratings and evaluations (online subscriptions or paper copies) or search online for product information to compare alternative goods even if you plan to make your final selection by shopping at a brick and mortar store. Of course online purchasing where possible could save both time and money from avoiding the need to shop at a traditional store. Shipping charges often are offset by lower prices on the items offered online.
  - o Some subscription services, such as *Consumer Reports*, offer new and used car pricing information that can be extremely useful and often can be used by people without regular subscriptions, though possibly at a slightly higher cost.
  - o For durable goods that you are likely to have for years (cars, electronics, appliances, furniture, etc.), it is a very good idea to look at the consumer guides that are available as long as the source is totally independent of any producer or retailer.

Some non-shopping specific ideas:

- If you live alone, consider getting a roommate to share expenses. If you already have a roommate, consider getting another one if you have the room. This is a particularly good idea if you are a young, single person just starting your career since you probably will spend a lot of time at work or socializing outside of your home.
- If you get a job near where your family lives, consider living with them **only if** you and your parents agree that you will live at home just until you find a place of your own, or to save some money until you can afford to move out or buy your own home. Don't simply take advantage of your parents' generosity. Instead, use it as a great opportunity to save as much as possible and to hone your own life skills.
  - o If you do end up temporarily living with your parents, pay rent. It is a really good idea to pay a reasonable rent and your share of utilities and groceries. Why? Because if you were on your own you would have these expenses, probably at a much higher cost, and it is not good to get used to "free living." The shock later can be overwhelming and may inspire you to stay at home longer than you or anyone should.

    Also, do your share of chores and do your own laundry. Not only is this an appropriate demonstration of gratitude for your parents' generosity, but this also will help you get used to adulthood responsibilities that you will need to know how to do once you are on your own.

Note To Give Your Parents

If you let me live at home after I graduate and get my first career job, I agree to pay rent, an amount that we both agree to that also covers my fair share of utilities and an additional amount of money for my share of grocery costs. I also agree to set a finite time for living at home that you agree with. If you don't want or need my financial contribution, then please save the money I pay you and use it as an incentive for me to go out on my own sooner rather than later. Do NOT give it, or any part of it, to me until I actually move out. I will probably want to renege on this, but don't let me. I am sure I will thank you later, probably much, much later, but I will eventually understand that this was in my best interest.

- Entertainment on the cheap. There are actually a lot of things to do that are relatively low cost. For example:
  o Go to a park with friends to play on free facilities (Frisbee, tennis, volleyball, etc.) or just to walk and hike on trails, or ride bikes on bike trails.
  o Have friends over to play board games or cards, and have everyone get in the habit of bringing their own liquid refreshments and a snack to share with others.
  o If you don't already do this, watch movies at home. Again, invite some friends over. Make this a casual party, but, again with the b.y.o.b. and snacks condition.
  o Use your local municipal recreation center if they have one. It not only provides good indoor recreation opportunities, but also costs less than most gyms or private recreation centers.
  o You get the idea: get creative. For example, taking short day trips to places in your local area that no one, except tourists, usually bothers to investigate can be a fun small group activity. These, along with many other creative ideas you can probably come up with on your own, can save a lot of money from going out to bars and restaurants, which is OK for special occasions but can be very pricey if done too often.

- Eliminate or reduce costly habits, such as smoking, drinking, or gambling. All of these habits can be extraordinarily expensive and each has potentially significant physical and mental health risks. If you regularly partake in any of these kinds of activities, you should control (preferably reduce or eliminate) these expenditures. This can save an incredible amount of money immediately. For example, a chronic cigarette smoker can save $200-$300 or more per month by quitting, and probably a lot more in the long run due to savings in out-of-pocket healthcare costs, not to mention potential improvement in your quality of life. The old saying "everything in moderation" really applies here!
- Save on utilities.
  o Look for a programmable thermostat. While you are sleeping or at work, turn your heat down in winter 5+ degrees less than usual, and in summer turn the A/C setting up 5+ degrees so it will turn on less often. Also keep regular heat/AC settings 2-3 degrees lower/higher (respectively) than you are used to. Your body will adjust, and more or less clothing can make up the comfort difference.
  o Get rid of landline phones, though most people your age probably don't have one.
  o Review cable TV/dish expenses. Do you really need 500 channels, or even some of the premium channels?
  o High speed Internet with Wi-Fi capability. Bundling can save money if you tie this in with phone and cable, but check out low cost services for each separately and judge costs in terms of what you really need.
- Don't casually purchase or take in stray pets because they are expensive. Make this a planned purchase if you want pets, but consider all costs, both financial and emotional as well as time relative to the benefits (for both you and the pet), and restrictions a pet may make on where you live and how long you can be away from home.
- Gifts for birthdays and holidays. As a young adult, you will probably want to upgrade the gifts you give. But you don't have to overdue on this expense. First and foremost, determine who you really want to give a gift to and for

what occasions. Second, set a dollar limit on these expenditures per event or per individual. Remember, you can make a gift special in a number of ways without spending an exorbitant amount of money:

- o Personalize the gift. Think of what that person would like. Pay close attention to what they say in general conversation that may give you an idea: music they like, a book, even a magazine subscription. Or perhaps something you have that they have raved about.
- o Just a greeting card can mean a lot if it is carefully selected to fit the specific person you are giving it to. But if you send a card, make sure it gets to the intended person on time!
- o Some people in your life probably don't need "things" (parents, grandparents, etc.), but they would love a remembrance of some kind such as a card, phone call, or personal visit.

- Use of consumer services. Minimize the use of some services that can be both expensive and not totally necessary (the definition of "necessary" will obviously differ for different people). These can be started again when finances are in better shape. Some of the services you might be able to do without include:
  - o **Coffee, lattes, tea, special drinks of any kind.** Have you ever considered how much money you could save by simply bringing your own coffee or tea mug to work or even bringing your own coffee maker to work where you can brew you favorite blend? Trust me, you could save a lot of money!
  - o **Dry cleaning**. Some work clothes or more formal clothing may require dry cleaning, but if you are doing this for a lot of clothes that you could launder at home (or in a laundromat) then you may be spending a lot of money unnecessarily.
  - o **Cosmetic "refreshing."** This is a tough area to talk about since it is a very personal expenditure. But it is also an expensive one that may not be necessary or not need to be indulged in as often. This also includes products you might purchase for face, hair, or other body parts. If you really think you can't live without these products, then shop around for the least

expensive ones that are of acceptable quality.

o **House cleaning**. You can probably do this yourself with good time management.

o **Lawn service**. Same as house cleaning: do it yourself if you have the time and equipment.

o **Pay to have important things done right so they don't have to be done over**. These would be things you, friends of yours, or "cheap" labor would otherwise do, but not very well. Hiring a professional to do these things also may free up time that you could spend making more money: working more hours at your job, getting a part-time second job, pursuing a hobby that might bring in revenue, or spending more time with your family and friends, which might also reduce stress, etc. Some examples include:
   - Plumbing
   - Electrical
   - Carpentry (build a deck)
   - Auto servicing/repair
   - Appliance repair
   - Painting
   - Wallpapering
   - Etc.

However, if you or your friends have the expertise and time, then certainly do it yourself. But, be prepared to reciprocate when your friends need similar help.

Special Cases for Reducing Expenses

Special Case #1: Food Expense and Grocery Shopping

This is a big part of most families' monthly budget, and an area where expenses can be reduced significantly. The average American family unit spends approximately $6300/year on food: $3700 for food at home and $2600 eating out. [8] You could reduce this expense by altering your consumer behavior.

- **Eat out less**. Buy your own groceries and cook your own meals. This can save hundreds of dollars/month for people who are single or for a childless couple who both work and tend to eat out a lot. When preparing your own meals, not only is buying groceries almost always less expensive than eating out, but it also can be much healthier because:

o   You can make sure ingredients are fresh.
o   You can minimize calories, fat and salt intake.
o   You can control quantity served and also avoid waste. American families waste or throw out 14% of the food they buy. [27]
o   You can minimize the amount of bread and other "fillers" consumed at each meal.
o   You are more likely to have a better-balanced meal (fruit, vegetables, etc.).
o   This ultimately can help you save more money by spending less on diet-related expenses or medical expenses, which could be significant.

- **Plan your grocery shopping**. Try to make grocery shopping a routine. Shop at regular intervals (once a week, once every two weeks, etc.), but often enough to minimize secondary "pick-ups" at convenience stores (which generally have higher prices) and especially if the pick-ups require a special trip to the store. You also should consider:

o   Shopping at the same time and day of the week, making this one of the routines we talked about earlier. Plan this time and day so you are not shopping when you are in a hurry (to get home, to work, or an appointment, etc.), which will help you avoid buying the first item that minimally meets your needs rather than being exactly what you want or need.
o   Avoid impulse buying.
o   Never shop before eating. You will buy items you want at the moment because you're hungry, and this rarely includes healthier foods.
o   Write a shopping list for every trip. Not just groceries, but all the other products you buy at today's supermarkets as well: cleaning materials, personal care products, over the counter health-related goods, greeting cards and, at some stores, beer and wine.
o   Shop at the same store so that you learn where things are, which again will minimize the temptation to buy other products that you come across during a search for items on your list. This also will save you considerable time.
o   Save coupons and USE them. This may take some

organization of coupons at home.

o Buy retail store brands when possible, especially for basic products. After all, aspirin is aspirin is aspirin, and these products are almost always less expensive since the brands are not advertised or as heavily advertised as producers' brands.

o Many stores have rebate programs (e.g., for food or fuel discounts based on how much you buy at their store). If you shop at such stores regardless of their discount program, use the discount cards they offer since the prices they are charging for all goods include the cost the store incurs for these rebates. In other words, if you don't use the card, you will be paying for those who do!

Alert!

In a profit-seeking private enterprise, nothing is free. If you see "free delivery," "free warranty," or, for that matter free anything, it translates in business-speak to "we have included the cost of that feature in the price of all goods we sell."

Special Case #2: Purchasing Durable Goods

These are products that are more important to you: more personal emotional investment in use of the product as well as style and status (self -image). They also reflect a larger part of your budget for monthly expenses (or your net worth if it requires you to take money out of savings or use debt to make the purchase). These are purchases that will last longer and cost more than perishable goods and services; thus, there is more risk involved in purchasing the wrong item. For these items, you should follow the buying process below:

• **Determine if this is a "need" or a "desired" purchase**. You can delay a desired purchase, which will give you more time to do a thorough search. However, to allow adequate time for purchasing "perceived needs," you should try to anticipate such needs. That will give you more time to search for and evaluate products to determine which one best meets your needs. But, before you start a search for a replacement product for something you already have, ask yourself these two questions:

o If it's broken, could it be fixed? Would the cost of repair be significantly less than a new product and does the new version of the product offer something the old one doesn't?

o If the problem with the old product is that it doesn't look good, or is not up-to-date, could it be updated so that you could get more useful life out of what you have? Of course, you should get estimates on the cost of such updating and compare that with the cost of a new replacement product.

- **Set specifications**. If you decide to proceed with the purchase of a new product, you should determine the specific parameters for your product search (price limit, features needed or desired, extended offerings such as warranties and delivery, availability of financing, etc.).

- **Conduct a search for alternatives that at least minimally meet all your specifications**. Start on the Internet, but also use RBWA (research by walking around) to stores that carry the goods. Observe similar goods you see at a mall, place of work, your neighborhood, talking to friends, co-workers, neighbors and family who have bought a product of the type you are looking for in the recent past. However, be aware that you should take personal recommendations with a grain of salt. Many people rationalize their purchases to avoid buyer's remorse, so you should ask specific questions about what they like best about the product they bought, or what problems, if any, they have encountered, or dislikes they have found after actually using the product.

This stage also should include consideration of *used or pre-owned products* that might meet all your needs at a significantly lower cost, especially if there is a seller's warranty offered with the used good. Products that tend to fall in this category are things such as autos, bikes, furniture, electronics, and especially little used exercise equipment—all of which often have very reasonable resale price tags for goods that are in very good shape. The warning here is that you should have any used product you are considering looked at by an experienced repair person if the product cost is at a level that would result in a financial problem if the product turns out to have defects or if no warranty was offered. Thus, always be sensible when buying anything advertised "as is!"

- **Evaluate the most viable of the products and services found in your search** (those that best meet your specification). Then in this stage, do a specific comparison of the final two or three best options. By doing this carefully, you usually can avoid a big mistake, since any of the alternatives you are now looking at should minimally meet all your needs. You are at this point trying to determine which can offer the greatest value: meet your needs well at a good price.
- **Next, decide whether or not to purchase any product.** If you do decide to purchase, then purchase the one that best meets your specifications. If none of the final alternatives fully meet all your needs at an acceptably high level, you should delay the purchase and start a new search, but only *if you anticipated this need/want ahead of time.* This option won't exist if you are buying for an immediate need.

  If you decide to go ahead with a purchase, then you should begin negotiating price, financing (if needed), delivery, etc. If the item is a "desire" rather than a need and you don't have the cash to pay for it, seriously consider postponing the purchase until you have the funds. If you have to obtain financing for a "needed" item, then seek out alternative sources for that financing. Often the dealer selling the product offers to arrange financing, but they may not offer the best rate. Instead:
  o Try your bank or insurance company. They often have the best rates.
  o Check loan rates online for the type of product being purchased.
  o If the dealer offers a no interest installment loan for 6, 12 or more months, this can be a very good financing option IF you are absolutely sure you can pay the loan off before the end date stipulated in their offer (new laws require a minimum payment each month for such offers); i.e., if you can save additional funds each month (beyond the minimum payments you make) in

order to be sure that you can pay the full loan balance off prior to the stipulated end date of the special offer. If the loan is not paid in full by the end date, the seller or their financing agent can add all the interest for the previous months of the loan to the balance due! If you need to borrow money to buy a product, make the biggest down payment you can afford from your current savings, without depleting the safety net amount of savings (this will be discussed later).

If you consider leasing, do not do so if you are simply trying to obtain a more expensive product than you otherwise can afford (car, furniture, electronics, etc.). Lease only to get a better payment for a product you can afford to buy and only if:

- You can meet all conditions of the lease (e.g., mileage limits on leased cars).
- Save the difference from leasing and purchasing in order to have the option to buy the product at the end of lease or to have a larger down payment for a new leased product.

You would be well advised to not lease any unnecessary products, such as new electronic goods. It's better to buy a gently used product in cash or keep the old product until you have the money to purchase a new one.

- **Evaluate your purchase**. Did it meet your specifications at the level you expected? If you are suffering from "buyer's remorse," then you may not have gone through the buying process as carefully as suggested. However, if you have a specific complaint or problem with what you purchased, take it back to the place you bought it as soon as possible. This is another reason why you should *always* keep receipts for durable goods, at least until the return and exchange period is over as well as the warranty coverage period if there was a warranty. If in doubt, keep receipts for these goods for at least one year. A good idea is to keep all such receipts in the same file, or electronically scan them into a computer file.

Special Case #3: Purchasing Consumer Services

This is a special case of purchasing since the goods you are buying are intangible (all services have some tangible element, but they are primarily intangible and perishable). This could include: renting goods for you to use (e.g., car rental, lawn equipment, etc.), or the servicing of goods you own (electricians, plumbers, house cleaning, lawn care, car servicing, etc.), or a more personal service (e.g., medical, dental, eye care, legal, physical therapy service, etc.). If purchasing services, you should consider the following suggestions:

- As noted earlier, expenditures for services should be made only when you do not have the appropriate expertise or when you can better spend your time earning more money (beyond what the service costs), or to achieve other important life goals, such as spending more quality time with family or friends.

- Treat service purchases the same way you treat other purchases: determine your specific service needs, search for information on the type of service provider you are looking for using references from friends, relatives, coworkers, neighbors, independent sources such as Angie's List (a subscription service), or even the yellow pages in the phone book or online. But look for professional certification and indication of bonded workmen or women (if not included on their advertisement, ask when you talk to them). Also check with your local Better Business Bureau for complaints filed for that service contractor.

  o Evaluate the two or three service providers that seem to be able to meet your specific needs the best. Ask for references or, in some cases such as a contractor who is going to do remodeling, ask to see samples of their previous work. The more significant the expense, the more thorough your search should be. For major service projects, be sure to get estimates with a guarantee ("no more than" clause). For most services, there is a wide range of estimated costs. Some may be lower but may not include "add-ons" that might arise after the work starts.

  o Decide whether to use any of the service providers you have evaluated. If it is not an immediate or emergency service need or you didn't find any provider that seems to meet all your needs, then continue the search. If you are able to select the one you think can do the best job for the monetary estimate they gave, then proceed, but be sure to:

- Get a definite start date (and a "finished by" date where applicable).
- Get your estimate in writing.
- Read any contract carefully before signing.
- Regarding payment for big projects: Don't agree to pay any more than 1/2 to 1/3 (preferably less) of the contract price as a down payment prior to any work getting done, and only in cases where it is clear that the service provider has to purchase some materials or equipment before they can start. Pay the remainder at the completion of the project or in installments as the project progresses. However, never make the last payment until the job is done to your satisfaction.

- When possible, share your post-service purchase experience with the same sources you used to help find the best service provider. You should be fair but honest in that evaluation.

Special Case #4: Purchasing "Big Ticket" Items

These are the items that, for the most part, you will purchase once or, at best, a few times in your life. They not only are the most expensive purchases you will make in your life, but also usually the most important to you in defining who you are or have become. Few people are able to pay for these purchases in cash, so they usually will have a very significant impact on your monthly expenses in terms of mortgage(s) and loan payments. Of course, ideally, you should plan your finances to be able to save or invest in order to purchase some of these major items in cash, particularly the ones that are not as clearly durable as some others (e.g., a wedding vs. a house).

Non-tangible major purchases: These are items that have a limited life for the actual event and are not as tangible as other major purchases, though they may change your life in a meaningful way. Two of the possible purchases in your life that fall in this category are:

- **Weddings**. An important symbolic and, for many, religious recognition ceremony that is often one of the greatest expenses you or a family member might incur. The non-emotional advice is to think carefully about this expenditure, particularly in terms of alternative uses of the funds needed for the event. So, apart from the emotional excitement of this event, some financial advice that you may or may not want to consider includes: set an absolute dollar limit that you are willing to spend; consider a small wedding with family and closest friends, with a simple reception for a larger circle of friends (a backyard, or public park event). Announcement of the wedding can be sent to an even broader audience.

  For parents, or others paying for this event (including the wedding couple), suggest putting anything from the dollar limit that is not spent into a savings account for the couple. But, try not to use all the money saved on an extravagant honeymoon. Also you may want to wait until later to take your honeymoon. Some people think it is good to wait a while to take such a trip—not right after an exciting, but often exhausting run-up to the wedding and, of course, the wedding day itself. On the other hand, if you or your families have the funds and, after careful thought, want to spend the money, then enjoy!

- **Additional education or training**. This is an increasingly important part of many young, and not so young persons' lives; something that can make a huge difference in lifetime earnings. Here we are assuming you already have started a career but have decided to pursue additional training: getting the college degree you never earned, getting a graduate or professional degree, or getting specific skills training. These purchases are not as tangible as other goods in that the results vary by individual, but at this point in your life, whatever education or training you may have in mind should be able to directly help meet your career and life goals. If not, it should be considered a personal luxury and categorized as an emotional want rather than a need. Financial advice to consider before making this kind of purchase includes asking yourself: 1. What is the cost of the type of education or training you are interested in? 2. How much financial aid is available? 3. What current savings are you willing to commit? 4. What employer contribution, if any, is available? 5. Are there scholarships or fellowships available, and if so, how much? 6. How much debt would you have to incur to pursue the education or training you want? 7. Are you willing and able to incur that debt? 8. What would the monthly payments be to repay the debt? In order to make a final decision on whether to incur this major expense, also ask yourself the following questions:

o How much are you willing to spend or borrow to purchase the education or training you are considering?

o What is a reasonable, conservative estimate of how likely you are to increase your income from successfully completing this education or training, and would that financially justify the expense?

o Do you have the time and personal commitment to complete this effort? A partial degree or incomplete training will do almost nothing positive for most people, financially or emotionally.

o Will this affect your ability to perform well at your current job?

o Are your significant other and family supportive of this pursuit and the costs that would be incurred?

Tangible major purchases: These are items that are expensive and that you probably will have for a long time, thus high risk goods for which you need to make rational financial as well as emotional decisions. This category includes those goods for which you not only spend a great deal of money—whether from savings or incurred debt—but also which fall in the category of "dreams" or "things you've always wanted." Thus, they usually are considered to be "desired" wants rather than "needed" goods. Desired wants include:

• **House or condo**. Yes, houses are not "needed." We can rent houses, condos, or apartments. In fact, after the housing market bubble burst in 2008, many financial advisors suggested that renting might be a better financial option for the millennial generation. On the other hand, some people still consider houses to be an investment and expect an increase in value over time or want one to fulfill a desired lifestyle.

- **Vacation home**. Some would consider this an investment, but that has not proven to be true in all cases—particularly timeshares—and, as with all homes, changes in value usually vary between regions of the country and world.
- **Luxury car**. Certainly not needed, but for many people a long-standing desire for self-image, status, or just to feel good. But this is, in most cases, an expense not an investment, so consider just how important this is to you, particularly if you need to borrow money in order to purchase this product.
- **Boat**. Unless you work as a fisherman or own a water-based entertainment or vacation service, this is a luxury item and often an expensive one both to purchase and to maintain.
- **Precious gems and jewelry**. This may fall into the category of investment if the jewelry is very high quality. However, there is no guarantee of increased value, and it doesn't earn any income during the time you hold it. Therefore, this also falls into the category of "want" and only should be purchased with cash. The one exception many people might suggest is an engagement or wedding ring. Retail jewelers often suggest some multiple of monthly income as the appropriate price range to consider and offer financing. Only purchase this item if you have the cash (and in the 2000's, it may be appropriate for both parties involved to share this expense). Even if you have the cash, consider how this money might go to better use for your future. For example, towards a house down payment. But, this may be one of the most personal, emotional purchases you have to make, so just be careful and think it through. Do not take funds out of long-term savings or investments to pay for such items.
- **Art and antiques**. These clearly are wants and might be a reasonably good investment IF you consult an expert

before the purchase. If you just like to have these objects for decorating, be very careful about how much you spend, and do so only in cash that you have available, not out of long-term savings or investments.

- **Investments**. Examples include: securities (stocks, bonds, mutual funds), precious metals, real estate (speculative or rental property), and collectibles (some would put valuable art and antiques as well as precious gems and jewelry in this category)
- **Other**. You may have your own additional set of tangible "wants."

You should approach these purchases in a manner similar to the durable goods purchases discussed earlier, but these items require even more scrutiny and evaluation since they will affect your finances to a greater degree and, in most cases, for a much longer period of time. In cases where this is an optional luxury item (not an investment that might increase in value), you should consider paying in cash or delaying your purchase. For anything that you consider an investment, you should spend money only on things you can afford and are willing to take a loss on (managing investments will be discussed in a later section). For any major purchase that is a "want" (again, these items are rarely "needs" in the true sense of that word), you should do or ask yourself the following:

- Rank order your wants (referring to your life goals and objectives) in terms of most immediate desire to satisfy as well as your ability to purchase.
- Does the purchase item have to be new, or would a quality previously owned good achieve your objectives? Pre-owned products usually can be purchased at a much lower cost, which may be a good alternative for items such as luxury cars, which depreciate quickly in value.
- Is this product likely to go on sale at some point, or is there a time of the month/year that is better to purchase such products?
- Does the particular purchase you are considering need the help of a professionally trained or experienced representative? Conversely, do you have the knowledge to make a good decision without such help?

Once you have answered the above questions, you should:

- Carefully and thoroughly **set your specifications** for the purchase you are considering. Appropriate specifications will, of course, depend on the product, but every purchase should include a specification on your upper price limit.
- **Search for information** on this product to find viable alternatives. This is where an agent who specializes in this product may be very useful. You should be trying to find alternatives that meet all your specifications and that will allow you to narrow your search to the three or four best options.
- **Evaluate the final viable alternatives** you identified, looking for the best value relative to how well the good meets your specifications.
- **Make a decision on your purchase.** First on whether you found any alternative that meets all your needs (remember, these are purchases for which the search can be started over if the "perfect product" is not found), and if so, which one best meets your needs.
- **Negotiate the best purchase agreement.** The purchase of the products in this category almost always includes some room for negotiation.
- **Evaluate your purchase,** mostly as a learning process for future spending since purchases in this category are not usually returnable and may or may not be easily sold at the same price you paid.

Reducing Expenses: Long-Term Strategies

These are some things you can do to reduce your expenses relative to income over a longer period of time. The long-term methods are more strategic in nature, so these ideas may take more planning and a longer time to implement. The results may not be apparent as quickly as the suggested methods for reducing short-term expenses, but the impact can be much greater over time.

Downsize and simplify your life. Unless you have life goals and near-term objectives for "living big" and having all the material symbols associated with financial success in our culture, a great way to dramatically reduce your living expenses and increase your ability to save and invest is to downsize some of the material things in your life or to generally simplify your life. Reducing expenses long-term might include:

- **Rethinking the size and type of house you need**. Do you really need a house with more rooms than you use? Do you need the amount of land your house sits on, or do you need to live in an area with such high property taxes (unless the latter truly reflect better schools or other amenities important to you other than status or image)?

    o As young people, your generation has the opportunity to make your first decision with this in mind. You can avoid the problem of being "house poor," having less to save or invest but also less to spend on other things that may make your life happier and more satisfying, by purchasing smaller, less expensive homes. Don't forget, large houses not only mean bigger mortgage payments and higher taxes, but also greater upkeep expenses and time commitments if you have to do it yourself (utilities, yard care, house cleaning), not to mention the cost of furnishing all the rooms you have that you may not even be using.

    o Keeping up with the "Joneses," or your own high expectations, can be very expensive and, for many people, not very rewarding in the long run. Alternatives include: a smaller house; a condo rather than a stand-alone house (often more space for the same money); renting rather than buying.

    o A lease is much shorter and more flexible than a mortgage, and can't lose value; nor are you responsible for repairs or upgrades. Admittedly, renting does not develop equity, but if you invest the money saved from renting, you may be better off financially in the long run. But if you want to own a home, consider buying an older home that may need some work rather than a new one with all the current trendy bells and whistles. Remember, granite countertops are not a need, though they may be a desire.

    o If you buy a newer house, look for a better environmentally designed house, reducing utility expenses. Also consider buying a house close to where you work or play. This can minimize transportation expenses and make your life a lot easier (less commuting time) and probably healthier due to more walking and biking.

o   If your current home meets your needs, don't look to upgrade; rather, consider refinancing at a lower interest rate or for a period of years that would allow you to pay off that home prior to retirement. However, you should do this only if you can repay yourself the cost of refinancing in 2-3 years. Also, this not only can reduce the years remaining on your debt, but, if the interest rate you can obtain is low enough, you also might be able to reduce monthly payment (but the latter is not as important as reducing the years of debt since this can significantly reduce the total interest you have to pay on a mortgage).

•   **Buy or lease smaller, less expensive, and more economical to use cars.** Most cars are a pure expense, not an investment. A new car loses approximately 9% of its value the minute you drive it off the lot, and 50% after only 4 years. [24] On the other hand, when there is a shortage of used cars on the market (as there was in early 2013) used cars will be priced higher than usual, possibly making a new car a better deal. [15]

Overall, the status of an expensive car is not what it used to be: With credit availability, many middle-class people can purchase a luxury car if they are willing to budget that expense. Luxury cars today don't look as different or have significantly more high tech gadgets than regular mid-priced models. New technology takes just a year or two to appear in relatively standard models of automobiles. Increasingly, there is more status attached to driving an environmentally responsible hybrid or electric car than a traditional gas-fueled car, whether the car falls into a mid-priced or luxury category. Consider the following ideas in order to minimize your auto-related expenses:

o   If you have a second car, determine if it is necessary. Significant savings can be made over the long run by eliminating a second car. Savings include: the initial cost, gas and routine maintenance, repairs, insurance, and in some cases additional parking expense. If elimination of a second car is not possible, then consider a less expensive but high quality pre-owned car that you can keep for ten years or more. In a dense urban area, consider a hybrid or electric car (obviously, good used ones will become more available as more consumers buy new ones).

o   If you live in a high-density large metro area, consider not using your car or, better, not even buying one. Rather, consider using less expensive transportation: walk or ride a bike where and when possible; use mass transit where available; or get into "share a ride" or car-pooling for travel to work. There are many local websites to help you find some of these opportunities with strangers who live near you, but first seek coworkers or friends you know who live near you and go to the same or nearby location as you do each day.

Note

Both mass transit and ride-sharing can become a good way to meet people, expanding your social circle, or to relax rather than fight traffic on days you don't have to drive (less stress), or even to get some work done on the way (managing time).

- **Reconsider how many luxury items you need.** You may "want" a boat, vacation home, expensive fashions, jewelry, etc., but are they really a necessary part of your desired lifestyle? "How would you use the good?" is the first issue you should question before making a luxury goods purchase. Would just owning it make you happy, or would it be used for a purpose that could justify the expense? What are the costs associated with keeping these goods? In some cases, the cost associated with owning goods such as a boat are significant, while the costs of owning a vacation home might be lowered if that home is located where there is a vibrant rental market for vacation homes. However, this does not guarantee rental income, and the wear and tear on that home may compromise the home's value. You also should ask yourself what the "opportunity costs" are of the money you spend on luxury goods, particularly those that are likely to depreciate in value over time. For example: you could have reallocated that money to additional savings, investments, or professional development, all of which could actually improve your net worth and future financial security.

- **Carefully review travel and entertainment desires.**
These are areas that reflect personal preference but are also categories of activities that can be expensive. At the same time, they should not be overlooked; these activities give you a break from work and from routine activities at home. They often are helpful in reducing stress as well as building relationships, and as with all categories we have discussed, they need to be planned. The following are some suggestions to think about in order to accomplish the "rest and relaxation" or "recreation" desires that you may have, but you also should consider the financial implications.
  o These expenses need to be part of your budget to ensure that you reserve funds for either regular or periodic entertainment, which may involve travel.
  o For regular travel and entertainment desires, you need to look at your budget and establish a monthly figure that is consistent with your priorities. While it is important to relax and enjoy yourself, for most people this category of activity is a "want" and not a "need;" thus, it should be one of the last items to plan in a budget.
  o For special entertainment or travel plans, such as a once-in-a-lifetime trip, you should make that part of your near- or long-term savings plan. If you designate a portion of your savings for these events, you hopefully will be able to pay for such travel and entertainment in cash, which should allow you to enjoy these activities much more than if it was purchased with any kind of debt.
  o As noted in a previous discussion, this also is a part of life that can be simplified and where expenses can be minimized. For example, consider "stay-cations" rather than vacations. They often are more relaxing

since you can stay home or close to home, minimizing travel expenses and hassles. The trick to making this work is to plan interesting places to go and not to intersperse work duties or household duties during these vacations even if you sleep at home each night. Also try your hardest to keep your cell phone, notebook, tablet, and laptop off, or even leave some of them at home. You may feel naked without these attachments, but you may get used to the freedom of not being connected 24/7/365.

- **Change your overall consumption behavior forever**. As with many components of life and financial planning, you need to make basic changes in your buying behavior over your entire life. For example:
  o Where possible, use cash (debit cards, checks). If you don't have the cash at the time, then save more or designate future savings in order to make that purchase. If the item is considered an actual necessity and not a want, then taking money out of savings may make more sense than buying on credit.
  o A possible acceptable alternative, as noted earlier, would be a special financing offer, such as a no-interest for 6 months or 12 months offer. But even then you should do this only if you are absolutely sure you can pay that purchase in full prior to the end of the specified time period.
  o Minimize use of credit cards for your purchases. Using credit cards when you cannot pay the total balance in the next billing cycle is the fastest way to get into financial trouble (see section below on managing your debt).
  o Buy higher value products (price, quality and durability), but then keep them longer, preferably for the useful life of the product. However, this usually will require planned savings specifically for purchasing these products.
  o Try not to buy anything that is too trendy. You won't keep it as long as something more traditional.
  o Don't buy "new-to-the-market" products until they have been on the market for at least 6 months to a year. This is the period when most flaws appear and

are corrected for the next version of that product; i.e., there may be a cost to being one of the first people to own the new gadget!

o   Higher quality products not only last longer and usually require fewer repairs, but, if in need of repair, the quality of these products also often justifies repair rather than replacement.

Managing Your Debt

Before reading the rest of this section, it would be a good idea to go back and see how you answered the questions in the personal finance quiz in Figure 1. You should focus on how you answered the questions that dealt with debt. Hopefully, the answers you gave in that quiz will provide an incentive to pay close attention to this section of the book.

The best way to manage debt is to not overspend and to stay well within your monthly budget in order to increase savings and investments consistent with your long-term financial plan. This may require you to change your lifestyle or at least question whether your current lifestyle is on track to meet your overall life goals. Of course, another debt avoidance strategy would be to find ways to make more money. But this alone will not always do the job of avoiding debt. Many of the bankruptcies and home foreclosures in the U.S. are for families in the top 20 % of income (over $100,000 per year). So, clearly, you need to focus on keeping spending within your monthly budgeted income.

Since this book is focused on Generation Y, you may be young enough, wise enough, or simply lucky enough to have avoided large amounts of debt, but the statistics on debt suggest that many have not (only 22% of your generation has no debt, and there is no good info on who specifically is included in that group). At the same time, the "great recession" that began in 2008 had a positive, though possibly temporary, impact on the overall household debt of people under 35 years of age in the U.S. Prior to the recession, average household debt for that cohort was approximately $22,000, but by 2010 it had fallen to $15,500. [12] Only time will tell if this reduction in debt was due to increased financial discretion, or due to loss of employment, fear of losing a job, or inability to get a loan. We can only hope that permanent lessons were learned during that financial crisis.

Sources of Debt Problems

There are many legitimate reasons for people to incur debt. It may be the only way to pay for higher education or training; it might reflect a need based on a personal or family emergency (e.g., a health care or legal problem); or for unanticipated repairs for necessities such as your primary car, refrigerator, stove, furnace, water heater, etc. While, in the long run these are things you should save for in order to be able to pay cash when such problems arise, if you don't have the money available, you may feel compelled to use debt.

Credit Cards. For most people, this is the most dangerous form of debt. Credit cards are easily available to most people, easy to use, and more frequent use of your card is encouraged by reward plans that offer cash or other rewards based on usage. But, unless you have an excellent credit rating, you may be paying an extremely high interest rate for any balance due that you don't pay off each month.

Credit card balances should, if humanly possible, be paid in full each month, and used primarily for convenience, safety (not carrying too much cash), greater ease in resolving disputes with the seller of a product that doesn't work or was misrepresented, and record keeping for monthly expenditures. If you religiously pay off your balance every month, then the interest rate becomes a moot point for you. But, if you are not self-disciplined and one of many people who seek immediate gratification for wants as well as needs, you can get into financial trouble very quickly by using credit cards.

Financial problems from misuse of credit cards tend to lead to a downward credit cycle over time. First, you may find yourself paying the minimum due on your cards, which will dramatically increase both the interest you pay and the time it will take to pay off that debt. If you find you are tempted to pay the minimum due on the card with another card, you now may be in serious financial trouble. Get help immediately from your bank or a local non-profit credit counseling agency. If you can't make a payment at all, you should contact the credit card company and explain your circumstances to get an agreement to pay less than the minimum, or possibly to lower your interest rate (more often than not, this is something better negotiated by a credit counselor). And, as true for all debt, the more of it you have, the lower your credit rating becomes, and slow pay or failure to pay on an account will further reduce that rating, resulting in denial of future credit applications or much higher interest rates. You can see how quickly the downward cycle can occur.

You can help yourself by avoiding special offers. Store cards frequently offer a percent-off merchandise purchase if you sign up for a new card, and bankcards may offer a temporary low percent if you sign up for their card and transfer other accounts to it. All are bad ideas because you end up with more cards than you need and more temptation to buy things you don't really need and can't afford.

Installment Loans (other than home mortgages). Buying a new product with an installment loan may be a case of hedonistic gratification or buying for a product want (as opposed to need) that you could and should delay until the older product is paid for. And even then you would be better advised to wait until you can pay in cash. On the other hand, if the product you are replacing is a real need, then first consider having the current product repaired or buying a good used product in cash.

As noted earlier, for some durable goods, such as automobiles, buying good quality used ("pre-owned") products can make more sense than buying new ones, even if you need to take out an installment loan. For any product that is prone to depreciation, which is most durable consumer goods, if you can find a well maintained, pre-owned product, you can get it at a very good price and avoid much of the depreciation of value, which is usually highest the first year after initial purchase. Using this purchase method, you can either get a much better product than you could afford new, or get a product you would normally be able to afford but at a much better price (and, thus, lower monthly payment). If, however, you decide to finance a durable goods purchase with an installment loan, check out loan rates at sites such as **bankrates.com**.

College Loans: A Special Case. College loans may be the only way to get the education you want, but after graduation (or stopping out/quitting college) they rapidly can become a major debt problem. Unfortunately, these loans are never forgiven and cannot even be erased in bankruptcy. If you have government-sponsored loans, the lender can be quite persistent in getting paid, even garnishing your wages for repayment. So, if you are still in school, be sure to use these loans only for expenses directly related to your education in order to minimize the debt load you will have after college.

If you are near graduation, or have graduated already, you should consider consolidating your college loans. But do this only if:

- You can find a lower interest rate than the current average rate of your loans.
- You have changed your spending habits to avoid developing new debt (it may be hard to find a really good loan rate if you currently have excessive debt).
- You pay down the debt consolidation loan at a high enough level to pay it off as soon as possible in a specified period of time. In other words, you should be paying as much or more than you were previously paying for the total of these loans before consolidating at a single, lower interest rate.

Note

The following is one of many web sites to consult for loan consolidation:
http://www.bankrate.com/finance/college-finance/college-loan-consolidation-101.aspx

---

You should note that, in some cases, college loans sponsored by the government (federal and possibly some state governments) might be reduced or eliminated by choosing certain kinds of jobs after graduation; e.g., Peace Corps, AmeriCorps, teaching in designated low-income areas, practicing medicine in low income areas without sufficient access to medical care, etc.

If you choose to consolidate loans to achieve a lower monthly payment, this could entice you to use that savings to buy more things you want. Unless that expenditure is an absolute necessity, and partly the reason to consolidate loans, you should avoid that temptation. If you do use the monthly savings from loan consolidation for anything but responsibly paying down the total loan, it could make this whole process a debt reduction failure and, worse, could lead to more debt. (You might feel that you have room in your budget to take on more debt.)

Mortgage and Home Equity Loans. Buying a house has been part of the "American dream" for decades; a dream that was realized for many Americans in the middle class. For years, home ownership was the single biggest and trusted investment for the average family, with an almost certain increase in value over time and an immediate benefit in the form of a tax write-off for the interest paid on the mortgage loan. However, after the housing market crash in 2008, some people are rethinking this dream. Housing values and prices fell dramatically, resulting in many people owing more on their mortgage than their house was worth (underwater mortgages). With the loss of jobs and income during the concurrent recession, many people faced foreclosure proceedings on their homes.

While a sad tale for those affected, there are important lessons to learn; not the least of which is that you should think long and hard before buying a house. Are you going to stay in the area for at least 5 years? Is the location you are looking at trending up or trending down economically? Are you prepared for all that goes with home ownership: house and yard upkeep, maintenance and repair, homeowner insurance, etc.? You should compare owning to renting, including what rentals are available, at what rental prices, in the locations in which you want to live. Of course, while renting can be advantageous, it also has a downside: renting does not build equity, you are limited in what personalized touches you can add to a rental property, your rent can be increased each year, and you may be charged a fee for breaking a lease if you want out of your contract for any reason.

If you are intent on buying a house, you should pay attention to the lessons learned from the recent experience of others. For example:

- If you want to maintain, if not increase, the value of a home, think more about location than the size or style of the house you buy. Also, do not buy the most expensive house in the neighborhood; it will have a much lower chance of increasing in value.
- Do not buy a "fixer upper" unless: 1. you can get an extremely good price on the property relative to others in

the area; 2. you or your family and friends are very handy and can do the work yourself (at a high quality level of work); and 3. you will have the time, patience, and out-of-pocket funds to get the necessary work done.

- Pay as much down as you can. At least 20% of negotiated price, plus a good credit rating, will usually get you the best interest rate and avoid a mandatory mortgage insurance premium from the lender. Shop for the best interest rate. Search online or go through a mortgage broker.

- Use conventional or FHA mortgages with the lowest fixed interest rate you can obtain for a 15-, 20-, or 30-year loan (the shortest period will save the most interest paid over the life of the loan). Do not fall for the "creative financing" schemes that caused much of the problem for homeowners who found themselves unable or unwilling to pay their mortgage during the recent housing market fiasco. These include: 1. land contracts or "rent-to-buy" offers, where you buy from the current owner; 2. interest only loans where no equity is built up with payments; 3. adjustable rate mortgages (ARMs) which offer a lower payment initially but are likely to increase over time, which can increase your payment dramatically;* and 4. balloon payment mortgages, where you pay a smaller monthly payment for a few years but then owe the entire balance at the end of that period, which either will have to be financed at whatever rate you are able to get at that time or paid off in full.

---

*Note

Adjustable rate mortgages should only be considered IF the initial rate is very low and there are clear and acceptable annual as well as lifetime caps that will prevent future ARM rates from going too high.

- As a young person who is not likely to stay in the first house you buy for more than 5-10 years, you probably will be encouraged to take the longest term loan possible (usually 30 years) on a mortgage. It will lower your monthly payments, but in the long run you would be paying much more interest (which would become less useful if there is any change in the tax laws for mortgage interest deductions on personal income taxes). This might allow you to buy the largest or most expensive house that you can get at a given level of payment. But remember, the shortest term mortgage you can afford is the best financial move in order to increase your equity in a house as much and as soon as possible since more of your payment goes towards equity, rather than interest, than it would on a longer term loan.

If you own a home and have some equity built up based on the down payment you originally made and the equity portion of the monthly payments you have made since the purchase, then this can become a basis for an unsolicited, relatively low interest rate home equity loan or an unsolicited home equity line of credit offer from your bank, loan company, or others. However, be very careful with such loans since they are based on your signing a second mortgage as collateral for these loans to guarantee payment. Thus, failure to pay on a home equity loan could initiate foreclosure on your house. Therefore, only consider such a loan if your income allows you to pay this additional monthly payment easily within your current budget AND you are using the proceeds from the loan to either consolidate other current installment loans that are at a higher rate of interest or to purchase something that maintains or adds value to your home; for example, a new HVAC system, a room addition, etc. Interest on home equity loans may be able to be deducted on your federal income taxes if you itemize deductions. However, this kind of loan should NOT be used for perishables such as a family vacation, not even a trip of a lifetime, or a good that depreciates quickly such as automobiles. For these more perishable expenditures you should use savings or a traditional installment loan, which is a more appropriate and safer method of debt.

Short-Term Loans. If you have a good credit rating, checking or savings accounts with a bank, and a steady current income, you may be able to secure a non-collateral short term loan to handle emergency or unanticipated expenditures for a product or service you need that cannot be covered by your current savings; or you don't want to deplete your savings to cover this expense. Using savings is almost always preferable to a loan (unless the loan rate is lower than your savings interest rate, which is unlikely), but using short-term bank loans is much more preferable than using credit cards unless you would be able to pay off the credit card balance in the next billing cycle.

There are other sources for loans, but they should be avoided, if possible. For example:

- **Non-bank loan companies.** These lenders target customers who cannot get loans from banks, at least not without collateral equal in value to the loan. There are "store front" loan companies and "tax refund loan" stores (who base loans on the borrower's copy of a 1040 or state tax filing form, showing a refund due). These lenders exist in most urban, and even some small town locations; often prey on low income people, asking for high discounts on the loan proceeds or very high interest rates; and are usually very aggressive at both selling their services and, in the case of loans, at obtaining repayment.

- **Personal loans from friends or relatives.** This might seem like a good source for a short-term loan, but as noted earlier, this kind of loan often has undesirable consequences. You should only ask for or accept personal loans when there are no other alternatives. Personal loans from friends and family often lead to bad feelings, potentially leading to permanently harmed relationships if you don't pay back such loans within the time period agreed to (or make payments as agreed to with the lender).

  You might be tempted to pay these debts last among other obligations since they usually are hard to enforce (often not having a legal contract) or maybe the lender can't bring themselves to take legal action. However, you should consider these loans as important a priority as any other debt obligation. Show how earnest you are as a borrower by delaying purchases for anything else that is not absolutely necessary other than regular monthly expenses until this debt is paid in full. Also, keep your personal lender informed if you can't pay on time, and have both an honest and reasonable excuse, as well as a plan on how to repay the debt.

- **Loan substitutes.** These usually are called and sold as something other than loans and sometimes are more of a loan in disguise. For example:
  o Cash rebates offered that you pocket rather than add to the down payment for the good you are purchasing on an installment loan (you should do the latter).
  o Pawnshops. These might be good places to buy some things, but you should never pawn valuable items. If you are planning on getting these goods back, the repurchase price usually is much higher than what you were able to "borrow." Essentially, it is equivalent to a very high interest rate on the amount you originally received from the pawnshop owner.
  o "Paycheck into Cash" centers, which cash paychecks for people who want their money as quickly as possible (usually people without bank accounts or direct deposit for paychecks) or offer cash for a personal check and hold them, for example, up to 14 days for a discount on the original amount. This discount usually is high and may lead to a cycle of spending money before you have it, possibly making it difficult to ever get ahead of that cycle.

Develop a Debt Plan

Hopefully, you paid close attention earlier and have already developed a monthly budget that allows you not only to live within your means, but also to save money. Now you need to develop a debt plan that will help you minimize or even avoid new debt (except for those items that most young people need and are unable to purchase without debt: houses, cars, etc.) and to reduce and eventually eliminate all debt.

In order to manage future debt, you should develop a financially sound personal and family culture. You need to review your life goals as well as financial goals and determine what is really important to you, including what debt-related expenditures are true "needs" and which are "wants." Thus, when considering purchases, you should develop a habit of only buying wants when you have the money available. You also should consider trying to save to buy wants when that is feasible, avoiding the "immediate gratification" tendency that so many Gen Y-ers demonstrate. You should look at this as "earning" these desired material goods, as a personal reward to yourself for accomplishing your financial and life goals. You may not believe this fully, but you will appreciate these purchases much more if you didn't have to go into debt to acquire them.

To reduce or eliminate current debt, you need first of all to review all the debt you have and then develop a debt reduction plan. If you are a "credit card junkie" or are on your way to becoming one, then establish a withdrawal program. Here are some basic ideas to get this under control:

- Minimize the number of credit cards you have. Keep only one or two bankcards, get rid of store cards all together, and have no more than one or two gas cards. Call and cancel the other cards, then cut them up. The fewer cards you have, the less tempted you will be to buy on credit wants or needs that can be postponed.
- Primarily use credit cards for:
  o Emergencies. Medical or dental emergencies, for example.
  o To have a record of purchases that you can and will pay off in full when the next credit card bill arrives.
  o To facilitate returns and refunds for goods you purchase. These often are easier if you paid with a credit card than with cash.
  o Convenience and safety when used instead of carrying cash. But, again, only if you pay off the balance due every month.
  o As a last resort for purchasing absolute needs for durable products that will last at least 5-10 years, without which you and your family would suffer and possibly incur substitute expenses. An example would be a clothes washer or dryer that cannot be repaired and you do not live near a laundry facility. However, it obviously would be better to use savings or a no-interest 6-12 month loan sponsored by the seller if you can pay the balance within the stipulated time period, or even a bank loan. A credit card should be used only if none of those options are available.
- Select cards that have no annual fee, low rates (if you will need to carry over your card balance for more than a month), and rebates (cash rebates are best). If you pay off

the balance due each month, the interest rate becomes unimportant.

- If you currently have a credit card balance that you cannot pay in full at the end of the month, stop making any further credit card purchases unless it is absolutely critical, and make sure that you pay more than the minimum balance each month until you can eliminate this debt. Even saving less per month in order to pay off this type of debt should be considered.
- Use installment loans sparingly, only for those critical needs that you could not afford otherwise.
- You should make sure that payments for these purchases are budgeted as part of your current financial plan. Before buying, set absolute maximum payment and length of loan limits that fit into your budget for each item that falls into this category. For example:
  o Home mortgages
  o Auto loans
  o Education loans
  o HVAC systems
- Shop around for the best interest rate for your installment loan. Start online, but also check with your bank, other local banks, your insurance company, etc.
- If, for any reason, you can't make a monthly payment, immediately contact your lender. Also review your current budget to see where else you can reduce expenditures, at least temporarily, without causing undue harm to you or your family; areas such as entertainment, travel, vacation, savings, and investments if necessary.
- If, on the other hand, your financial plan is going well, then voluntarily make an additional payment towards the principal on your loan each month, reducing both the duration of that loan and the amount of interest you will have to pay over the life of the loan. You even may want to reduce savings in order to pay down this debt if the interest rate on your savings is less than the interest being charged on the loan.
  o Try to avoid any personal loans for reasons mentioned earlier. The best way, of course, is to be disciplined financially, saving and investing each month so that

you can pay for unplanned expenses. Or, postpone any purchase or spending that is not an absolute need until you have the funds. This also gives you time to better determine if you really want the item in question.

- For all types of debt, remember:
  o It may be tempting to pay a loan off as slowly as possible, but that may not be a good idea. The slower you pay, the more dollars of interest you are going to pay.
  o Debt will lower your credit rating, keeping you from getting the best rate on future loan needs as well as insurance rates, and that could even affect an employment application.
  o Get help if you need it, both to do debt planning and to implement your plan. When seeking help, avoid uncertified credit counselors, and if possible, avoid profit-seeking credit counselors. There are very good non-profit credit counseling organizations that will either not charge anything or have a minimum charge for their help. And beware: many financial planners are not qualified debt counselors.

Managing Savings and Investments

A key element of financial stability and, ultimately, financial success is to save and invest as much money as possible. If your monthly budget does not allow any savings or investment beyond minimum tax-deferred retirement contributions, then you need to either go back and reconsider your other expenditures to see where those can be reduced, or it may be time to change your lifestyle to allow you to begin to save and invest until your income can be increased to afford that lifestyle.

You need to force yourself to save. That should be one of the highest, if not *the* highest, priorities in your financial planning other than being able to pay for your most basic necessities and debt repayment. Remember, savings should be viewed as a regular monthly expense.

Short-Term Savings and Investment Plan. You need to have some cash savings (in an interest-bearing savings or money market account) and other relatively liquid accounts such as short-term certificates of deposit. This provides you both a safety net for unanticipated events not reflected in your monthly budget and allows you to purchase some wants and needs in cash rather than having to borrow. However, you should review periodically your short-term savings to make sure you are not keeping more than necessary in these accounts since the rate of interest earned is usually much less than on longer-term investments.

If you are unable to save enough per month to develop a reserve "cash fund," you should make sure you have reduced all possible areas of spending and, as a last resort, consider a reduction in the amount you are withholding from your paycheck for tax-deferred investments and retirement plans. However, you should do this temporarily and only until you can find better ways to increase your regular savings reserve. If you have neither savings nor long-term investments, then you need to seriously consider changing your lifestyle as quickly as possible.

Short-term savings should be designated for:

- A reserve for loss of income (layoff, loss of job, injury to you or significant other). This portion of your short-term savings should cover a minimum of 3 months of living expenses, but preferably 6 months given the recent history of how long, on average, it takes unemployed people to find a new job. It should cover an even longer period if you are single, or have a significant other who is not employed or who is susceptible to a layoff or sudden loss of job.
- Short-term wants, such as a TV, notebook computer, vacations, etc. to avoid using debt, especially credit cards, for those wants.
- Unanticipated or emergency expenses so you can survive the unexpected without financial difficulty. These include uncovered medical, dental, or vision emergency expenses and unexpected repair costs for car, home, appliances, etc.

Long-Term Savings and Investment Plan. Long-term savings should be primarily in the form of investments in order to earn income from savings to achieve long-term financial goals, while minimizing the need to use debt to pay for long-term wants and needs. Long-term savings and investments should be used for:

- Major purchases for which you have planned to save in order to pay cash or at least minimize your debt requirements, such as a house (or a second house, cottage, or major home remodeling) or advanced education for kids, spouse, or yourself.
- Economic crises, like the recent housing market crash.
- Financial independence; not letting money be the primary or only factor in your life decisions.
- Retirement. In addition to Social Security or company "defined benefit" retirement programs, which are rapidly becoming a thing of the past, retirement savings should be, whenever possible, in tax-deferred long-term investments such as 401k or 403b programs, or in an Individual Retirement Account (IRA).

Long-term investments require due diligence from you, the owner of the account; however, in most cases you would be well advised to consider the use of a professional financial planner, making sure he or she is a "Certified Financial Planner." In any case, you do not, as they say, want all eggs in one basket, having all your investments in one stock, including the stock of the company you work for or own. In fact, you don't want just stocks, but also bonds and cash (money market) and possibly real estate. In most cases, it would be best to have your investments in indexed mutual funds, which are going to better meet inflationary trends and will automatically create a degree of diversity in your investment holdings. At the same time, you don't want to have all your long-term investments in one mutual fund. It may have a balanced investment within the fund, but each individual mutual fund may perform differently over time. Thus a balance of funds by type and parent company should make your investment safer than using just one fund.

You also should consider "stage of life balance" in your investment portfolio. Different financial advisers may offer some variation in the specifics presented below, but generally:

- **Young adults** early in their career should have a heavier balance of investments in stocks (60-75%) than bonds or other fixed-income investments. And depending on your level of risk aversion, generally stocks can and should be in a "growth" category. Young people can withstand downturns in the market since time is in your favor (you have time for such losses to be reversed) and your portfolio can recover and continue to grow.

- **Middle-aged adults** in the middle of their career should have a portfolio with 50-60% stocks, with the bulk still in growth stocks/funds, but with some portion of your portfolio in bonds and less risky stocks.
- **Late-middle-aged adults** (pre-retirement or "career change") should start reducing the stock balance in their portfolios to 40-50%, and have less of their funds in growth stocks.
- **Retirement-aged adults** will need to have at least 30-40% of their investments in stocks, though the exact amount will depend a great deal on your overall financial situation and age at retirement.

Note

You should consult other sources of investment advice, either books or, better, a certified financial planner who can determine the best investment plan for your particular circumstances at each stage of life.

Tax-deferred long-term investments are recommended by most financial counselors. Your investment will grow faster and the tax rate you will have to pay in retirement will likely (but not always) be less than what you pay during your peak earning years. One of the downsides is that you may have a limited number of approved investment vehicles to choose from in your employer sponsored 401k or 403b investment program,* though some firms offer a wide variety and allow the individual investor to rebalance their portfolio of funds periodically. Another downside is that you cannot cash out any part of these investments without withdrawal penalties from the investment management company, and you will owe income taxes on those withdrawals. However, in most cases you can borrow from tax-deferred plans for specific purposes such as buying a house or education expenditures, but you have to pay these loans back at a stipulated interest rate.

---

*Note

The company(s) that your employer approves for tax-deferred investment plans will usually have financial advisors available to help you plan your investment strategy.

Another possible form of potentially tax-deferred investment is an IRA. People your age can invest up to $5,500 per year in an IRA, as of the 2013 tax year, that can be deducted from federal taxes IF you qualify (there are income limits: see IRS Publication 590, Individual Retirement Arrangements). In any case, distributions from an IRA cannot be taken (without penalty and taxes due if contributions were deferred) until age 59 ½. For people whose income restricts them from using a "deductible IRA," they may qualify for a "partially deductible" IRA, and others may still choose to use an IRA even if it is non-deductible for them, since earnings in the IRA are not taxed until you begin taking distributions from that investment. There is also a Roth IRA option, where the contributions are made from after-tax income, but the earnings are not subject to federal tax when distributions are taken from that investment. But again, there are income restrictions on who can benefit from this option.

Non tax-deferred investments might be a better source of funds for purchases that are part of your long-term financial goals other than retirement. These funds can be accessed relatively easily and usually without withdrawal penalties; and you only have tax liability for earnings on the investment, not on the principle since the investment was made with after-tax funds. The downside, of course, is that this investment won't grow rapidly if you continuously use part of it for purchasing goods and services that may not be necessary. On the other hand, if these investments were placed in non-tax-deferred accounts in part to have such funds available for your wants, that is OK, and much better than borrowing money for such expenditures.

Depending on your desired personal level of involvement, alternative approaches for this kind of investment include:

- **DIY investing.** You can "Do It Yourself" for non-tax-deferred investments, but you should do so only if you have developed investment expertise and you are willing and able to devote the necessary time and effort to do this without affecting your other life goals, such as family and social life. The best method for investing in individual stocks and bonds is probably online trading through a recognized online brokerage firm. However, for most individual investors, you might be best advised to select different mutual funds in which to invest, particularly focusing on "no load" (no fee) up front funds, with low annual maintenance expenses charged by the fund— usually a percent of your investment. Mutual funds are by definition diversified within a category (e.g., a variety of growth stocks, both U.S. and foreign), and it is a good idea to invest in a variety of mutual funds, each with different market focus.

- **Licensed brokerage firm.** The broker will recommend buys and sells, though you make the final decision. If you use this method, you should develop a relationship with a specific representative of the firm and stay with that person over time if your portfolio performs as well as you expected. But a warning: these firms may have certain stocks and bonds they are pushing, more for improving their own bottom line than yours.
- **Banks (usually discount brokers).** Some bank brokers can be quite good, but they may not be as well informed as other professional brokers, though their commissions are often much lower. Consider this if you are personally well informed on the securities market but do not have the time to do it yourself.
- **Certified financial planner.** This is a good method for those who have little personal experience and want to work with someone who is not tied to any particular company that may have its own investment objectives. They only earn money if your portfolio earns money. Certified financial planners usually take either a percent of your portfolio earnings or have a "fixed" fee. They also offer help in developing an overall financial plan, thus are particularly useful not just to those near retirement, but also for younger people who want to begin their road to financial stability and success. (For ideas on how to find a certified financial planner see the following article:

http://www.cfp.net/utility/find-a-cfp-professional/).

Additional Savings and Investment Issues. The amount to save or invest per month depends on a number of considerations. Depending on your financial objectives and goals, you should try to save a minimum of 10-15% of after-tax income; possibly more if some of your designated savings is in the form of tax-deferred investments. Your initial plan should put more emphasis on your short-term cash or liquid savings. If you do not have at least 3 months of expenses saved in a cash account, you need to put all your savings per month in that account until you reach the desired savings level. When you do, then you can start to put half of your monthly savings into tax-deferred retirement savings. Be advised, you may only be able to opt into this type of program at certain times of the year, depending on your employer. You should place the other half of your monthly savings into your cash accounts until you have an amount equal to 6 months of regular expenses in that account. After you have achieved a level of savings in cash or liquid accounts equal to 6 months worth of expenses, then begin to put half to two-thirds of your monthly savings into your tax-deferred investment account and start placing the rest in a non-tax-deferred long-term investments discussed above. Or, use part of the latter to purchase some want or need that you deferred until you had the money to purchase that good or service.

Once you achieve your basic safety net cash savings, try to maximize your tax-deferred investments, especially if your employer matches what you place in such investments (usually up to a specified maximum). If they do not have such a program, then proceed as suggested above.

Some investment hints:

- Review and rebalance your investment portfolio at least once a year, if possible with the advice of a financial planner or investment adviser unless you have made investing a personal hobby. If you don't have a portfolio, start developing one!
- For the vast majority of young investors, you should consider indexed mutual funds, both stock funds and bond funds, or balanced funds. Again, unless you want to make a perpetual study of the markets a second occupation or

avocation, it is best to pay for good, trustworthy investment advice from a certified financial planner or professional financial advisor for both your tax-deferred and non-tax-deferred investments.

Some savings hints:

- Develop your own monthly escrow for known upcoming expenses. In other words, instead of having just one savings item in your monthly budget, divide that into several sub items, such as new car fund, new computer fund, etc., for anything that you know is a near-future expense that you want or will need to incur. This can help you avoid using credit cards or loans, or to minimize the necessary amount of a loan you may need for such purchases.
- Save the change you have left over every day in a jar. If possible, do the same with $1 bills. This small change or bills jar can become part of regular savings or used for extras like going out to dinner. Americans collectively have an estimated $7.5 billion in coins stashed away in piggy banks, socks, coffee cans, etc., and approximately $8000 in coins get thrown in the garbage per day.
- If you have young children, start them on the right financial path. Give them an allowance, but make sure they save some reasonable portion of their allowance so that they develop a savings and "pay in cash" habit; as well as learning to develop financial goals and plans for achieving those goals.

Implementing Your Financial Plan

Although good planning is absolutely necessary for financial success, it is not sufficient. You actually have to implement your plan and, as with most plans, that isn't always easy. Once your plan is finalized, you still must do the following:

Develop a "reasonable" timetable. You need to decide when to start your plan. As indicated earlier, the ideal month to begin your budget is the first month of a new salary year or the beginning of a tax year (for most of us that is January). But you don't have to wait. Set a start date, and then begin to record your actual expenses per month. Review all your expenses and determine how to reduce current expenditures, where possible, in the short or near term. In other words, set a "to be done by date" for yourself.

Create your monthly budget. This next step should be based on a review of expenses. Then set a start date for the new budget. After starting to use your budget, keep a record of your actual expenses to determine how well you are staying within your budget for each item. Keep track of the exact amount you spend, indicating how much it is above or below the budgeted amount. After no more than two months of using the new budget, you need to evaluate how well the budget, as a whole, is working and make any necessary adjustments, though you should try to keep monthly savings as planned in the original budget unless there is no other way to make your revised budget work. Keep track of the revised budget each month. You will get better at it over time, and it will become part of your weekly or monthly routine. Of course, every time there is a change in income (hopefully an upward change), you need to revise your budget. Hopefully, you also will recognize this as a good opportunity to increase savings or tax-deferred investments withdrawn from your paycheck.

Over time, as you find new ways to reduce your spending and pay off debt, you will again have to revise your budget, but this should be a more positive chore, determining how to spend or save the additional funds resulting from your financial planning effort. As a Generation Y reader, this should be fairly easy for you to do with the aid of either money management software or developing your own computer spreadsheet. By now you are probably figuring out that budget revision is a never-ending process. In the end, it's totally up to you if you want to be in control of your finances or let them control you.

8. Related Financial Issues

Protecting Your Financial Position

It won't benefit you or your family (present or future) to have done a good job of financial planning if you fail to take the necessary steps to protect you financial achievements.

Insurance

This is the first protection method that you should consider; something that almost everyone hates to pay for but is usually a necessary expenditure to protect your assets and, therefore, yourself and significant others over time. However, there are many kinds of insurance, some of which are often part of an employer-sponsored benefit plan and some that are not. Some types of insurance should, in most cases, be considered "must haves" whether or not they are part of your employee benefits. Others are more optional, but also should be considered.

"Must Have" Insurance:

- **Health insurance:** For you, your spouse or significant other, children, and maybe parents. In addition to basic healthcare coverage, also consider prescription, dental, and vision insurance.
- **Life insurance:** Often, but not always, offered as part of an employee benefit plan. It's important to have whether part of such a plan or purchased independently. If you wait until you are older, the premiums may be much higher.
- **Automobile insurance:** Required by law in most states, automobile insurance should be considered a "must have" since a devastating car accident could cause you to forfeit all your assets not only now, but also in future years.

- **Disability insurance:** Another must have for anyone who has not yet become eligible for Social Security disability. A catastrophic illness or injury could prevent you from working for years, even the rest of your life. Some employer benefit plans include this, but you should consider purchasing this as an "add on" to your company plan or do it independently if it is not automatically provided.
- **Homeowners, condo, or renters insurance:** Again, you could lose a significant investment in an owned house or condominium if you incur a major uninsured loss. Usually you mortgage company or homeowner's association will require minimum homeowner insurance (and rental companies often require renters insurance).

"Optional" Insurance (but should be considered):

- **Long-term care insurance:** Although this is usually thought of as a concern for older people, there are two reasons a young person should consider this: First, the younger you are when you purchase this insurance, the less expensive it is, and second, sometimes bad things happen to young people. No one is immune to serious illness or accidents that could require this kind of care.
- **Liability insurance (umbrella policy):** This kind of insurance can protect you from liability for a variety of issues, including unintentionally causing harm to other persons, either at home, work, or elsewhere. A claim or lawsuit for personal harm can involve hundreds or thousands of dollars, or more in some cases. This insurance is usually quite reasonable, cost-wise.
- **Travel insurance:** For major personal trips planned, it might be wise to purchase travel insurance to make sure funds you are committing for such travel will not be lost for reasons beyond your control, such as illness or weather.

Other Insurance Considerations:

- **Should you insure your children and a stay-home partner or spouse?** Health insurance on all dependents is usually considered essential since you have financial responsibility for medical expenses incurred. For life insurance, you should consider insuring a stay-home partner or spouse who is performing a great many tasks at home that would cost a great deal of money (or time) should they be unable to perform those activities. But it also may be important to consider insuring a child's life in order to get life insurance at a very reasonable cost that can be transferred to them when they become independent. However, you should make sure there are clauses for voluntary increases in the amount of coverage.
- **What is the best way to find the insurance you need or desire?** If insurance is not covered by an employee benefit plan, then you should shop around for the best rate on the insurance coverage you need. Go online to shop for rates (see **www.insurancequotes.com**) or find an independent insurance agent in your locale that handles insurance policies for a variety of different companies.

Wills

There are two types of wills that are particularly important in regard to protecting your assets for both you and your significant others:

- **Last will and testament:** This is necessary, especially if you have dependents, to make sure that your accumulated wealth in money and belongings is transferred to those to whom who want to leave it, and with minimal difficulty and expense, avoiding or expediting probate procedures. Even if you are single, you may want those things that you worked hard for to go to the people or organizations of your choice. You can find general template forms for developing your own will online, but you probably should have a lawyer look over the document, if not develop it for you in the first place, to make sure it meets legal requirements where you live.

- **A "living" will:** This ensures you have a say in what extraordinary procedures you want to endure if physically or mentally incapacitated, and to whom you want to give authority to make decisions for you. You may want to include a provisional power or attorney for whomever you trust to take care of your financial responsibilities if you are unable to do so and either have no legal significant-other or that person does not feel they could handle such a responsibility. Again, this is something where a lawyer could help you.

Protect and Improve Your Credit Rating

You should try to establish and maintain a good to excellent credit rating: a FICO score over 700, preferably 760 or above out of a possible 850 points. [3] This is not just important to be able to get a loan when you want or need to, but it also may affect the rate of interest you are able to obtain on various loans. A good credit rating also is important for housing or apartment rental applications, and insurance companies increasingly are using credit ratings as part of their determination of rates to charge customers. In addition, some employers use credit scores as a method of determining prospective employees' record of responsibility as part of their hiring decision.

You may have heard from other people that to develop a good score you need to establish a record of credit (installment loans, credit cards, etc.). This is somewhat true, but needs to be qualified. Having several (1-3) credit cards is probably a good idea (for example: one bankcard, one gas company card, and possibly one other bank card as a back-up in case something happens to your primary card). But having too many cards may be a detriment to your credit rating. Not only are they an opportunity to overuse credit card debt to buy things, but even a responsible person who doesn't use them or pays off the balance each month on all cards, also is harmed simply because they have that credit available to be used, thus lowering your score. By the way, if you already have more cards than you need, don't close your accounts too quickly because that also can harm your credit rating. Instead, close them one by one over time and not prior to seeking a longer term installment loan.

Other factors that may be taken into account in a credit rating include:

- Not paying bills on time, particularly regular monthly bills such as mortgage or utilities.
- While it may not seem fair, stability is also a factor. Job hopping as well as moving your residence too often may affect your rating.
- Of course, your net worth (accumulated wealth) is also a major factor. Obviously a low or negative net worth would hurt your credit rating.
- Be sure to check your credit report at least once a year to make sure everything is accurate. Take advantage of your right as a U.S. citizen to get a free credit report from each of the three major credit reporting agencies each year: Experian, TransUnion, and Equifax. Go to **www.annualcreditreport.com** to do this. But beware, the credit reporting agencies may attempt to sell you additional services not required by the government. As of 2013, these agencies only have to provide a free report, and may charge you a small fee for reporting your numeric credit score (though it might be worthwhile to obtain that score if you anticipate the need to secure a long-term installment loan in the near future). Go through those reports very carefully to scrutinize each item to make sure it is correct. It might be smart to look at one of the three agency's reports every four months, rather than all three at one time. If you find an error on any report, immediately file an appeal with the credit rating agency. Specific contact with each agency can be made as follows:
  - o **www.equifax.com**
  - o **www.experian.com**
  - o **www.transunion.com**

Tax Planning

You could improve your financial position by reducing your tax obligations. Keep receipts for anything you think might qualify as a tax deduction. For example: charitable contributions, unreimbursed business or job expenses including moving costs, education expenses that are required for employment, etc. Note that some deductions may be taken without itemizing all deductions on your tax form (see IRS 1040 instructions if you do your own taxes). You also should keep track of any taxable income that will not be reflected on a W-2 statement from your employer. Although most other income may be provided on a 1099 tax form, you should keep track of cash income for tax purposes.

Also try to find ways to minimize taxes you owe. Take advantage of tax-deferred income opportunities such as 401(k) or 403(b) options that your employer may offer, or a Keogh Plan if you are self employed. This leads to forced savings and investments for retirement and also reduces your taxes. You also should consider putting money into a traditional IRA if your adjusted gross income qualifies you to deduct the contributions you make. Your employer also may offer a flexible medical plan that allows you to save money (before taxes are deducted) that is dedicated to medical spending. However, the money you put in these medical savings plans per year usually fall under a "use it or lose it" policy.

If you own a home and have enough equity built up, then minimize the interest cost of installment loans for major durable goods and services like home remodeling by using a home equity loan or line of credit that allows you to deduct interest paid on those loans from your taxes (with some restrictions). However, as warned earlier, using home equity loans or lines of credit involves a second mortgage on your house, and a failure to make your payments on such a loan could result in a foreclosure on your home. On the other hand, interest paid on regular installment loans is not deductible for tax purposes.

In any case, if you are a homeowner you probably can justify itemizing your deductions due to mortgage interest and the property taxes you pay that can be itemized. To help you find all possible tax deductions, consider using a tax accountant. Once a professional has done this for one tax year you may be able to do your own taxes with the aid of tax filing software programs, such as **TurboTax** by Quicken and **TaxCut** by H&R Block, that are updated each tax year.

If you are not sure if itemizing deductions will reduce the taxes you owe more than taking the standard deduction allowed, try doing your taxes both ways to see which results in the lowest tax due. Some tax software will alert you to which is better for your circumstances.

If you use the standard deduction allowed instead of itemizing deductions, you can file your federal tax form online with the IRS for no fee. However, if you itemize deductions, you will have to use the 1040 long form. If you have any of the following tax complexities you should consider using an experienced tax accountant: have rental property income; are self employed; are living and working in different states (or have homes in different states); have capital gains from investments that are not tax deferred; etc.

As a general rule, don't do your own taxes unless you are sure you know what you are doing. Even if your return is legally correct, you may have missed some tax savings opportunities, not to mention saving time and stress. There will be a cost incurred to have them done professionally, which should be in your budget.

Also keep your tax records, preferably in electronic files but in paper form if nothing else. You legally need to keep these for at least three but preferably up to seven years in case you are audited. It may be important for filing your taxes in any given year to have easy access to your previous year returns.

Common Financial Pitfalls to Avoid

Not Keeping Good Financial Records

Keeping financial records is a good idea beyond tax records and receipts that were mentioned in the section above. Make sure you have all important records and documents that you may need. Keeping records can affect your finances (able to return goods you bought) and help reduce stress in your life. For example:

- **Major purchase receipts.** You should keep any receipt for a durable good unless you can afford to replace it if you don't like it. Most stores set limits on how long you have to return a product without an original receipt. Over time this can involve a great deal of money for either product replacement or having to pay for repairs, since most warranties also require these receipts. If you keep manuals that come with most durable goods (and you should), staple the receipt inside the manual cover and put all manuals in a file drawer.
- **Bank records.** Many people, especially young people, do their banking online and have gone "green." Thus, these

receipts should be available from your online banking account. However, loan papers for mortgages and other installment loans are often voluminous and may not be available electronically. Keep a file of these loan agreements until the loan is paid in full. Keep the loan payoff document after the loan is paid in full. (Save that for at least a year.)

Seeking Unqualified "Professional Help"

Whether looking for a financial advisor, a debt counselor, an accountant, or a "life coach" (which seems to mean different things to different people), you need to make sure the person or organization you select to help you with your finances or other life issues is qualified. There are accreditation and licensing bodies that "certify" many of these professions. You should be aware that in many states people with little or no qualification can call themselves a financial advisor or counselor without being certified or even without a degree of any kind. In some cases this is also true of accountants, and certainly is true for debt counselors. In other cases, people with a degree in one field do work in another in which they were not directly trained; for example, lawyers touting their ability to offer debt counseling. They may be able to help with a negotiated settlement with the IRS, but may know little about other financial issues.

So pay attention to the old caveat, "buyer beware." Check out any potential counselor or advisor with the local Better Business Bureau and ask to see their actual certificates from their certification associations (and you probably should check to see if that is a valid organization). Today, a lot of investigation can be done online, but it needs to be done before you spend money for such help and certainly before taking their advice. This is why it might be quite useful to contact providers of these services whom your friends or relatives have used and can attest to their competence.

Of course, as noted earlier, you also need to be cautious when listening to a self-proclaimed "expert" speaker or author on a subject of importance to you. Check them out, and see what their qualifications are. If they are reluctant to tell you about or show you their diplomas or cannot verify experience in the field being discussed, they probably are not qualified. Worse, some of these folks simply have false credentials to display and do not hesitate to misrepresent themselves as an expert. A good way to sort this out is this: If any supposed expert is trying to tell you how easy it is, or how quickly you can solve a problem, then this is likely to be an unqualified or, at best, semi-qualified person. Run, don't walk away, and do not spend your money or time on these slick "quick fix" salespersons.

Unnecessary Warranties

Most consumer advocates, such as the Consumers Union, or independent product testing organizations, such as Consumer Reports (CR), with their paper and online publication of the same name, strongly suggest saving your money and not buying (literally) the extended warranty for most durable products. Most warranties, other than the basic manufacturer's warranty, are not cost effective for the consumer. Most products are made much better today than ever before, although many are certainly more complex, have more parts, and use a higher level of technology. But, the cost of warranties to the consumer often is high compared to the likelihood of needing covered repairs. For example, CR suggests that there is no need for extended warranties on most new automobiles for mechanical or electrical failures, nor for their paint protection or rust-proofing, which easily could add up to well over $1000 for the consumer. If temped to pay for this, consider putting an equivalent amount of money in a savings account and using it as necessary for repairs; most people will save a considerable amount of money from doing so over the same time as the length of the warranty offered.

For less expensive durable goods, such as a coffee maker or toaster oven, the need for a warranty is even less cost effective. Most people who buy these products with a warranty never have a problem, and those who do usually just buy a new replacement product because it is a hassle to pack up the product and send it or have to take it to an authorized repair center, and because it may be too inconvenient to be without that household product for possibly days or weeks. This is not to say that we should continue to be a "disposable" society, throwing things away rather than having them repaired. But if you know you are unlikely to go to that trouble, at least don't spend money on an extended warranty.

Compulsive Spending

This was talked about earlier but probably deserves another look. If you have to have every new product, style, or gadget, at least stop and think why. Do you really need it (in most cases it is a want), and is it worth the money you will have to spend? We all know people who have a desktop computer as well as a laptop, plus a tablet with Wi-Fi, and probably a smart phone also with Wi-Fi, and possibly a mini laptop for travel and maybe a separate e-reader. It is highly likely that one or more of those "absolute necessities" are not used very much and their functions could be performed on one of the other devices.

TVs are another great example of compulsive spending. Many people seem willing to spend whatever it takes (often on credit) to get the biggest, newest model with new features and functions without asking if they really need all those functions or if their current product is not meeting their needs sufficiently. Most household furnishings, electronics, and exercise equipment have a very low resale value on the used goods market, so spending money for a new item to replace one that works perfectly well is a type of compulsive spending. It might be that you want to be the person with the newest in-thing, or you might be trying to keep up with neighbors, family, and friends who were the ones who had to have the newest thing first. Rather than comparing your financial position, career, or possessions against what others around you have, compare where you are relative to your own life goals and how well you are meeting them today versus 6 months ago or a year or 5 years ago.

Find ways to avoid compulsive buying: find things to do other than shopping in stores or online; stop delivery of any mail or online-order catalogs that you don't need; do not go shopping without a list of predetermined purchases to be made and stick to that list. Shopping should not be the way you spend your free time but viewed as a chore that needs to be planned. It also is a good idea to always pay cash for items that are wants, or at least things not absolutely needed now. You will be more likely to think twice about a purchase if you are spending hard-earned money rather than using a credit card.

Not Assessing Your Risk Tolerance

Too many people risk money they can't afford to lose: gambling in casinos, getting involved in stock market activities such as day-trading, which is even risky for professional stock traders, or in a business venture that some friend, relative, or co-worker suggests is a business investment opportunity that seems too good to be true—and probably is just that. This is not to say that a well thought out business plan for a new entrepreneurial idea you have shouldn't be pursued, even if it includes significant risk. But, if you do pursue such a venture, it should be done in consultation not only with any significant other, but also with a qualified financial advisor before taking such a risk. If an opportunity is presented that has a short turn-around time for you to make a decision—too little time to carefully investigate the opportunity—then it probably is best to walk away.

Failing to Protect Yourself from Identity Theft

Identity theft has become a lucrative and illegal business not only in the U.S, but worldwide. One report indicated that "As many as 9 million Americans have their identity stolen each year." [16] If this happens to you, it can be costly. Checking and savings accounts can be drained, affecting your credit rating; credit cards and loans can be taken out in your name and then not repaid, also affecting your credit rating; or someone can file and receive a tax refund under your social security number before you file your own tax returns. All of these consequences could take many hours, days or months of your life to straighten out, and this often requires expensive legal help. In some cases it can be catastrophic financially and take years to just get back to where you were when it began.

So, take some precautionary steps to protect your identity. For example:

- Never provide your social security number, bank account, or credit card number to anyone or any organization unless you called them and absolutely know to whom you are speaking.
- Never put your social security number or account number on a document if it is optional. If it is required, call and ask why and only provide it if absolutely necessary.

- Don't throw away any paper document with private information or personal identification information, including account numbers and social security numbers, in the trash. A home paper shredder is one of the best purchases you can make. Very good ones for home use can be purchased for around $50, sometimes less.
- Check your bank and credit card accounts regularly. This has become much easier to do with online banking. Look at recent transactions and activity to make sure they are legitimate. If you see any that are not, call the bank or credit card company as soon as possible.
- As indicated in the section on protecting and improving your credit rating, check your credit report at least once a year, preferably more often, and any time that you find an error on the credit report (particularly a loan or credit card that you did not obtain), report it immediately.

If you suspect identity theft, you should contact your banks, credit card companies, the IRS and file a report with the Federal Trade Commission. You can get an official form to report identity theft as soon as possible by going to:

http://www.ftc.gov/bcp/edu/resources/forms/affidavit.pdf/

Even those who are very conscientious about protecting their identity can find that identity has been stolen. However, by following the above suggestions, it might help mitigate the damage that occurs since you are more likely to detect the problem earlier than you would have otherwise.

Note

If you have had an identity theft problem, it might be a good idea to sign up for more frequent credit report checks and alerts for a fee.

---

9. What to Do if You Get into Financial Trouble
Or, you were in trouble before you read this book.

Refer to Previous Sections of this Book

Go back and review some of the suggestions in earlier parts of the book. Most importantly, start to implement those ideas to the best of your ability, especially to assess your current financial position and develop a budget that you can live within; reduce your expenses where possible; pay off debt; and save some minimal amount of money each month. Also review your life goals and objectives to remind you of your priorities, including financial planning that is necessary to achieve those life goals.

Help is Available

What help you may need depends a great deal on your level and definition of trouble. If you feel that you are falling short of meeting either or both your short-term financial objectives and long-term goals and can't seem to develop a workable plan to establish a budget or to find ways to reduce your expenses or increase your savings and investments, then you may want to consider using the services of a financial planner. However, beware that most such advisors are private, profit-seeking professionals, so you want to make sure they are Certified Financial Planners. Also, you should be aware that such advisors usually are best qualified and most interested in offering investment advice, but many can and do offer general financial advice as well. These professionals often are selected based on referral from satisfied customers, so ask any of your relatives or friends who seem to have their financial life in order to recommend someone.

If you find yourself in serious financial trouble (can't pay bills, including rent or mortgage and other installment loans), get help immediately from debt counseling specialists:

- **Non-profit debt counselors.** Local non-profit debt counseling centers are the least expensive (usually free or very low cost) and can provide excellent service. They may charge a fee based on "ability to pay" or may not charge a fee at all, but were created to help people with serious debt problems, and, importantly, non-profit organizations see themselves as primarily working on your behalf. The national foundation for Credit Counseling provides a locator service for free or low cost debt counseling (**www.nfcc.org**).

- **For-profit debt counseling services** also are available and may provide a useful service, but they charge a fee for their service. This is either a direct fee or one based on a percentage of how much they can save you in monthly payments. They also may be paid by the companies they work with to consolidate your loans. However, these companies have a vested interest in how they help you, so always remember that nothing is truly free in private enterprise!

- **Banks** where you maintain checking or savings accounts, credit cards, and where you have taken out loans (particularly if they are the banks holding your home mortgage). They may help you with a lower interest rate or reduce your monthly payment to a more manageable level.

- **Some employers** offer financial counseling services for employees. If so, you should at least investigate such a service since there may be no charge or a minimal charge. However, you should get a guarantee of confidentiality since some of the information they will need may include some issues you would not particularly want to share with your employer.

- **Lawyers** who specialize in debt counseling and resolution might be helpful, but there is going to be a fee, possibly a considerable one. They also may encourage you to consider bankruptcy sooner than might be advisable. There are long-term credit consequences to bankruptcy, and it does not eliminate all debts. Most notably for Gen Y, this includes college loans.

- **Friends?** This is not a particularly good source of advice unless the given friend is a certified financial planner or has a personal record of great financial success that can be verified—and not just by how nice a house or car they have. Many people who look affluent have the greatest debt. Friends are generally most useful as a source for referrals to professionals with whom they have been very satisfied from a personal experience.

Warning!

If you find yourself in financial difficulty, seek help from a credible source, and do so sooner rather than later. Most financial problems can be solved, but the first step is to admit you have a problem and find someone who knows what steps to take.

---

10. Finale: Just Do It

Hopefully you have carefully considered the suggestions offered in this book. Certainly, there is no one right way to approach these very important life issues. This book attempted to offer a logical, holistic approach that combines major life and personal finance issues into one overall life plan. But, if nothing else, I hope that you will have accepted the one overarching idea of the book, particularly for your generation: that *there is no quick, easy or magic solution to achieving all that you may want out of life*. Regardless of the approach you take, you need to:

- Reassess your values.
- Determine short-term and long-term goals, including retirement goals.
- Develop a life plan, including a money and finance plan.
- Implement the combined total life plan.
- Periodically assess your plan and revise it if necessary.

Ultimately, planning your life, including your personal finances, should give you peace of mind so you can better enjoy your life. You can do it, but you should start now, while you are young.

Remember, if you don't just do it then nothing will change and you are leaving to chance whether you will be able to live the life you want. So, I won't wish you good luck, but rather successful planning!

Sources Consulted

1. Bureau of Labor Statistics, 2012.

2. Censky, Annalyn at CNN Money, "How The Middle Class Became The Underclass," reported at www.money.com/2011/02/16/news/economy/middle_class/index. html

3. Consumer Reports, "The Ultimate Money Guide," Consumers Union of U.S., 2007.

4. Godon, Joe, "Stress and First-World Countries." Reported at www.voices.yahoo.com/stress-first-world-countries-147715.html

5. Gose, Ben, "4 Massive Open Online Courses and How They Work." *The Chronicle of Higher Education*, at http://chronicle.com/article/4-MOOCsHow-They-Work/134664/

6. http://assets.newamerica.net/files/1109SavingsFacts.pdf

7. Hofer, Barbara K. and Abigail Sullivan Moore, "The iConnected Parent," Simon & Schuster, 2010.

8. Kelley, Pat, "The Average Monthly Family Food Budget." Reported at www.ehow.com/about_7344144_average-monthly-family-food-budget.html/

9. Lattin, Beth, "A Graduate Degree in Debt," Forbes.com – 03-10-09

10. Pew Research Center, A Portrait of 'Generation Next.'" January, 2007.

11. Pew Research Center, as reported in *The Week*, 12/14/2012

12. Struck, Heather, "Household debt falls sharply among younger Americans; study," Pew Research Center study, as reported in: www.finance.yahoo.com/household-debt-falls-sharply-among-younger-americans/152103198.html

13. Supiano, Beckie, "To Foster Financial Literacy, Students Need More Than Information…" *The Chronicle of Higher Education*, 2/27/2013.

14. Taylor, Chris. Reuters, Monday, Sept. 24, 2012, reported on *Yahoo! Finance*.

15. "The Smoking Hot Market for Gently Used Cars," found at http://business.time.com/2013/02/27/the-smoking-hot-market-for-gently-used-cars/

16. *Time.com*, as reported in "The Bottom Line," *The Week*, 12/07/2012.

17. "The ABC's of Generations Y and Z – What Defines These Youngsters?" Reported at www.premisemarketing.com/

18. *The New York Times*, as reported in *The Week*, 3/15/2013.

19. *The Washington Post*, as reported in *The Week*, 12/07/2012.

20. Yue, Cynthia, "America's Incredible Shrinking Savings Rate." Reported at www.businesscommunity.com.infogaphics

21. Wohlsen, Marcus, "Tuition at Learn-to-Code Boot Camp Is Free — Until You Get a Job." Reported at http://www.wired.com/business/2013/03/free-learn-to-code-boot-camp/

22. *www.cnn.com*, "Colleges Try to Contend with Hovering Parents." 8/29/2005.

23. www.ConsumerReports.org/College-Students-Have-Highest-Debt-to-Date/

24. www.edmonds.com/car-buying/how-fast-does-my-new-car-loose-value-infographic.html

25. www.ehow.com/about_5382164_long-aveage-car-loan.html

26. www.ehow.com/info_8367042_average-debt-college-students.html

27. www.foodproductiondaily.com/supply-chain/half-of-us-food-goes-to-waste.htnl

28. www.pewsocialtrends.org.files/2012/03/PewSocialTrends-2012-BommerangGeneration.pdf

29. www.statisticsbrain.com/AmericanFamilyFinancials-statistics/

30.www.uscourts.gov/uscourts/statistics/bankruptcyfilings/2012/1 212_12

Suggested Reading

Stress Management:
Greenberg, Jerrold S. *Comprehensive Stress Management.*
Leyden-Rubenstein, Lori A. *The Stress Management Handbook: Strategies for Health and Inner Peace.*

Time Management:
Felton, Sandra. *Organizing Your Day: Time Management Techniques That Will Work for You.*
Vurnum, Gary. *Time Management Techniques: 92 Affirmations That Apply Time Management Tips For Overcoming Procrastination.*

Career and Professional Development:
Lore, Nicholas. *The Pathfinder: How to Choose or Change Your Career for a Lifetime of Satisfaction and Success.*

Organizing Your Life:
Felton, Sandra. *Organizing Your Day: Time Management Techniques That Will Work for You.*

Health. Fitness, and Appearance:
Betta, Ron. *Outstanding You: Discover, Design and Achieve Ultimate Fitness.*

Personal and Professional Relationships:
Tamm, James W. *Radical Collaboration: Five Essential Skills to Overcome Defensiveness and Build Successful Relationships.*

Personal Finance:
Orman, Suze. *The Money Book for the Young, Fabulous, and Broke.*
Ramsey, Dave. *The Total Money Makeover.*
Stanley, Thomas and William Danko. *The Millionaire Next Door.*

Appendix 1
Glossary of Financial Terms

Bonds: Certificates that represent money a government or corporation has borrowed from individuals or organizational investors.

Certificate of deposit: Often referred to as a (CD) it is a "time deposit" (cannot be withdrawn within a certain period of time without penalty), offered to customers in the United States by banks, thrift institutions, and credit unions.

Collateral: A borrower's pledge to a lender of specific property to secure repayment of a loan, which protects the lender against loss from a borrower's default on a loan.

Home equity loan: A loan in which the borrower uses the equity in their home as collateral in order to finance major expenses such as home repairs, remodeling, higher education, etc. This type of loan creates a lien against the borrower's house and reduces actual home equity.

Home equity line of credit: This is a revolving credit loan, also referred to as a home equity line of credit, where the borrower can choose when and how often to borrow against the equity in the property with the lender setting an initial credit limit. Borrowers usually pay a variable rate of interest if and when they use all or part of the line of credit to make a purchase. If funds are borrowed, the equity in the borrower's house becomes collateral for the loan.

Individual Retirement Account (IRA): A form of retirement plan provided by many financial institutions that provides tax advantages for retirement savings. IRAs have both contribution limits and restrictions on eligibility, as described in **IRS Publication 590, Individual Retirement Arrangement (IRAs).** Traditional IRA contributions can be fully deductible, partially deductible, or non-deductible for federal tax purposes. The latter is based on income restrictions. Roth IRAs are not tax-deductible, but earnings from the investment are not subject to federal income taxation when the funds are withdrawn. The total tax deduction that can be taken for either a traditional IRA or a Roth IRA is $5,500/per year for anyone under 50 years of age.

Liquid assets: A financial asset that can be easily and quickly sold (or withdrawn), with minimum loss of value. Money, or cash, is the most liquid asset and can be used immediately to perform economic actions like buying, selling, or paying debt, meeting immediate wants and needs. Other than cash, money in checking, savings or money market accounts are the most liquid. Other securities, such as certificates of deposit, often are considered to be liquid since funds can be withdrawn relatively quickly, but possibly with loss of value due to early withdrawal penalty.

Money Market Account: This is a financial account that pays interest based on current interest rates in money markets. These accounts, often referred to as "money market deposit accounts," typically have a higher rate of interest than savings accounts, but require a higher minimum balance (anywhere from $1,000 to $10,000 to $25,000) to earn interest or avoid monthly fees. These accounts offered by financial institutions are FDIC insured.

Money Market Fund: A money market fund (also known as money market mutual fund) is an open-ended mutual fund that invests in short-term debt securities such as U.S. Treasury bills and commercial paper (short-term unsecured promissory notes). Money market funds are widely (though not necessarily accurately) regarded as being as safe as bank deposits yet providing a higher yield. However, they are not FDIC insured.

Mortgage insurance premium: Mortgage insurance (also known as mortgage guarantee) is an insurance policy, which compensates lenders or investors for losses due to the default of a mortgage loan. Mortgage insurance can be either public or private depending upon the insurer. Private mortgage insurance (PMI) is typically required when down payments are below 20%.

Mortgage: The word *mortgage* is commonly used as being synonymous with the term *mortgage loan*. A mortgage loan is a loan-secured real property through the use of a mortgage note, which is evidence of the existence of the loan and the encumbrances of that realty through the granting of a mortgage, which secures the loan. These loans usually are for a fixed period of time (15 years or 30 years are most common), with either a fixed rate of interest or a "variable" rate that is initially lower than fixed rates, but can go up or down over time depending on movement of bank rates of interest.

Mutual fund: A mutual fund is a type of professionally managed *collective investment vehicle* that pools money from many investors to purchase securities. While there is no legal definition of the term "mutual fund," it most commonly is applied only to those collective investment vehicles that are regulated and sold to the general public. They sometimes are referred to as "investment companies" or "registered investment companies." Most mutual funds are "open-ended," meaning investors can buy or sell shares of the fund at any time.

Stocks: The equity stake of the owners of an incorporated business, divided into shares (1 share = 1 unit of ownership). Common stocks represent voting shares, and preferred stock holders do have voting rights.

Tax-Deferred Investments:
  401(k): 401(k) plans are "defined contribution plans" with annual contributions limited. Contributions are "tax-deferred"—deducted from paychecks before taxes and then taxed when a withdrawal is made from the 401(k) account. The employee's contribution may be matched by the employer.

  403 (b): A 403(b) plan is a U.S. tax-advantaged retirement savings plan available for public education organizations, some non-profit employers, cooperative hospital service organizations, and self-employed ministers in the U.S. It has tax treatment similar to a 401(k) plan.

  Keogh Plan: Keogh Plans are a type of retirement plan for self-employed people and small businesses in the United States. There are 2 basic types of Keogh Plans: defined-benefit and defined-contribution plans.

Term life insurance: This type of insurance provides coverage at a fixed rate of payments for a limited period of time. After that period expires, the client must either forgo coverage or potentially obtain further coverage with different payments or conditions.

Whole life insurance: Whole life insurance is an insurance policy that remains in force for the insured's *whole life* and requires (in most cases) premiums to be paid every year into the policy. There are at least six types of whole life insurance; thus, one should consult a qualified insurance agent to determine the most appropriate policy to consider.

Appendix 2
Hints for Developing Values and Goals

Identifying Values: If, as with most people, you find this hard to do, begin by spending some time reflecting on what is important in your life:

- *Personal factors:* money and wealth, status, personal accomplishments, happiness, having fun, helping others, health, self-improvement, staying true to your faith.
- *Family-related factors:* relationship with immediate and extended family; having your own family (children); family members' health and financial well-being now and in the future, with or without you.
- *Friend-related factors:* relationships, fun, support.
- *Work-related factors:* salary, accomplishments, advancement, future opportunities, professional recognition.

Developing goals: It is a good idea to start with your highest level and longest term goals and work your way down to the more specific goals and objectives, making sure the latter are consistent with achievement of the higher level goals:

- *Life achievement goals:* The highest level goals one can have; becoming the person you would ideally like to be.
- *Retirement goals:* These are goals related to when you would like to retire, how you want to live after you retire, what you want to be able to do with your life once you are able to leave your primary occupation, and how much money you will need to live that life as well as to pay the additional costs associated with aging.
- *Long-term goals*: These are major directional goals that are necessarily less specific, but hopefully doable. These are important, but you should spend more time on short- and near-term plans that can achieve these goals.
- *5 year near-term goals*: These are specific, doable, and less limited (1 year objectives should lead to these).
- *1 year objectives:* These should be specific, limited in number to what is most important and doable; a few good

objectives. Focus on what is most important, and prioritize on the important objectives that can be accomplished in a year.

Appendix 3
Sample Time Plan
[Parameter = 168 hours/week]

Start by creating a general time plan, such as the one below. Then do the following:

- Modify the plan to specifically reflect **your** regular schedule of activities, making sure you dedicate time for relaxation (leisure, socializing, etc.) and break some hours into ½ hour slots if that works better. Modify your plan over time as necessary.

- Build flexibility into your time plan. For example, both "relax" and "optional" are times that can be used as flex time for any unexpected events or activities that come up, or as time slots to make up for other regular activities if those time slots had to be used for unexpected events or duties.

A.M.	MON.	TUES.	WED.	THURS.	FRI.	SAT.	SUN.
6:00	Get up / ready	Get up / ready	Get up / ready	Get up / ready	Get up / ready	Optional	Optional
7:00	Travel to work	Travel to work	Travel to work	Travel to work	Travel to work	Optional	Optional
8:00	Work	Work	Work	Work	Work	Optional	Optional
9:00	Work	Work	Work	Work	Work	Optional	Optional
10:00	Work	Work	Work	Work	Work	Optional	Optional
11:00	Work	Work	Work	Work	Work	Optional	Optional
P.M.	--------	--------	--------	--------	--------	--------	--------
12:00	Lunch	Lunch	Lunch	Lunch	Lunch	Lunch	Lunch
1:00	Work	Work	Work	Work	Work	Errands	Errands
2:00	Work	Work	Work	Work	Work	Errands	Errands
3:00	Work	Work	Work	Work	Work	Chores	Chores
4:00	Work	Work	Work	Work	Work	Optional	Optional
5:00	Work	Work	Work	Work	Work	Optional	Optional
6:00	Workout	Workout	Workout	Workout	Workout	Optional	Optional
7:00	Dinner	Dinner	Dinner	Dinner	Dinner	Dinner	Dinner
8:00	Chores	Chores	Chores	Chores	Chores	Relax	Relax
9:00	Relax	Relax	Relax	Relax	Relax	Relax	Relax
10:00	Relax	Relax	Relax	Relax	Relax	Relax	Relax
11:00	Go to bed	Go to bed	Go to bed	Go to bed	Optional	Optional	Go to bed
A.M.	--------	--------	--------	--------	--------	--------	--------
12:00-6:00	Sleep	Sleep	Sleep	Sleep	Optional	Optional	Sleep

Appendix 4
Sample Budget

2013	Budget	Actual Month 1	Actual Month 2	Actual Month 3	Actual Month 4
Gross income	**$40,000**				
Income after taxes	**$30,000**				
Liquid Assets:					
Checking Acct.	**$1,200**				
Savings Acct.	**$3,000**				
Other	**$0**				
Total:	**$4,200**				
Monthly Expenses:		Actual Month 1	Actual Month 2	Actual Month 3	Actual Month 4
Rent/mortgage	($650)				
Home maintenance	($0)				
Utilities:					
Electric	($50)				
Gas	($50)				
Cell phone	($60)				
Internet/Cable	($100)				
Other	$0				
Insurance:					
Auto ins.	($60)				
Health ins.	($80)				
Life ins.	($40)				
Homeowner/renter ins.	($20)				
Other	$0				
Auto Expenses:					
Car payment	($300)				
Gas/maintenance	($100)				
Public transport	($50)				
Parking	($50)				
Groceries	($300)				
General Spending	($300)				
Medical copay/deductible	($40)				
Misc.	($50)				
Loans/credit cards	($100)				
TOTAL EXP.	($2,400)				
NET SAVINGS / MONTH	$100				

Note: Set up a budget on Excel or another spreadsheet. Use "SUM" formulas for "Total Expenses" and for "Net Savings" (+ monthly income – total expenses). Then, using your own monthly income figures, record actual monthly expenditures for several months and modify the budget as necessary.

About the Author

James S. West is a professor of economics and business at Washington & Jefferson College. He has over thirty years of experience teaching college courses in marketing, management, and international business and also has consulted for both businesses and non-profit organizations. West holds a Ph.D. in Business Administration from the University of Nebraska and a Master of Arts degree, specializing in Economics, from Minnesota State University.

Brianne Bilsky is an administrator in the Office of Student Life at Washington & Jefferson College. She holds a Ph.D. in English from Stanford University and is a member of Generation Y.

www.ingramcontent.com/pod-product-compliance
Lightning Source LLC
Chambersburg PA
CBHW051506170526
45166CB00001B/407